Colonialism and Foreign Ownership of Capital

First published in 1982. Foreign control of capital is a major problem for many developing countries and can lead to the exercise of a form of colonial control whereby capital is provided for political rather than economic reasons. This book discusses the implications of this phenomenon for trade theory and the amount of pressure that foreign countries can exert. The opening chapter examines the themes of de-industrialisation, of stagnation after an initial spurt in economic activity, and the premise that inflows of capital do not necessarily generate growth and expansion. These initial discussions are developed in the subsequent chapters where the effects of foreign ownership on the host country's economy and trade are dealt with fully. This work would be of interest to students of economics and development.

T0382917

Colonialism and Foreign Ownership of Capital

A Trade Theorist's View

Bharat Hazari

First published in 1982
by Croom Helm

This edition first published in 2016 by Routledge
2 Park Square, Milton Park, Abingdon, Oxon, OX14 4RN
and by Routledge
711 Third Avenue, New York, NY 10017

Routledge is an imprint of the Taylor & Francis Group, an informa business

© 1982 Bharat R. Hazari

Publisher's Note
The publisher has gone to great lengths to ensure the quality of this reprint but points out that some imperfections in the original copies may be apparent.

Disclaimer
The publisher has made every effort to trace copyright holders and welcomes correspondence from those they have been unable to contact.

A Library of Congress record exists under LC control number: 82149544

ISBN 13: 978-1-138-64355-0 (hbk)
ISBN 13: 978-1-315-62932-2 (ebk)
ISBN 13: 978-1-138-64360-4 (pbk)

Colonialism
and Foreign Ownership of Capital

A TRADE THEORIST'S VIEW

BHARAT R. HAZARI

CROOM HELM
London & Canberra

© 1982 Bharat R. Hazari
Croom Helm Ltd, 2-10 St John's Road, London SW11

British Library Cataloguing in Publication Data

Hazari, Bharat R.
    Colonialism and foreign ownership of capital.
    1. Imperialism—Economics aspects
    I. Title
    337   HC59

    ISBN 0-7099-1241-2

Printed and bound in Great Britain by
Biddles Ltd, Guildford and King's Lynn

CONTENTS

Preface

To the Memory of my Mother

PREFACE

This book is based on a series of lectures I was
unofficially asked to prepare for possible presentation as the Raymond Parkinson Memorial Lectures
which are organised by the University of the South
Pacific. Rumour has it that I was not allowed to
deliver them due to the nature of racial politics at
the University. I was subjected to a racial assault
in July 1981, which naturally resulted in my resign-
ation from the University and premature departure in
December 1981 instead of June 1983. After this
violent incident I was asked if I would be willing
to deliver these lectures. Following the principle
that discretion is the better part of valour I
declined this request. Having discussed the rather
unusual history of this book, I now proceed to
discuss its contents.

This work is concerned with analysing the trade-
theoretic consequences of foreign ownership of
capital where the foreign country possess absolute
monopoly power in trade of capital. The latter
phenomenon is captured by assuming that the supply
of foreign capital is completely inelastic - in other
words it does not depend on the rate of return. The
quantity of capital supplied is determined on the
basis of political considerations by the metropolitan
country. In the case of colonial economies the
metropolitan country also controls the political
regime. The freedom to determine the quantity of
capital brought into the host country provides the
foreign owners with political and other leverage.

An analogue of the above assumption is
available in microeconomics, where in the theory of
monopoly, it is assumed that the industry consists of
only one firm. The motivation for attempting an
exercise on the basis of such a simple assumption is
to highlight the consequences of a specific type of

imperfection in an analytically easy manner, for both
positive and normative microeconomics. The assumption of absolute monopoly power in trade of capital
is also made partly for similar reasons. However,
its main motivation comes from the desire to capture
the effect of unequal trading power on the host
country. This work may be described as the
neoclassical approach to the recently developing
literature on 'unequal exchange'.

The opening chapter discusses three themes that
are frequently found in works on economic history
and development economics. These are (i) de-industrialization, (ii) stagnation after an initial spurt
in economic activity and (iii) that the inflows of
foreign capital do not necessarily generate growth
and development. These themes are initially
discussed on the basis of an exceedingly simple model
in which the host country produces two exportable
commodities. One of these commodities is produced
with the help of labour alone; unlike the other
which is produced with the help of labour and
inelastically supplied sector-specific foreign-owned
capital. All the earnings of foreign-owned capital
are repatriated - an assumption that is maintained
throughout the book. In this simple framework the
themes mentioned earlier are all confirmed. Several
new results are also obtained.

Chapter 2 generalises the above framework to
include another sector (importable good), another
factor (domestic capital) and another distortion
factor price differential. Several results of
Chapter 1 are re-confirmed on the basis of this more
general model. Several new results are also
obtained. For example, it is shown that the removal
of the distortion is not necessarily desirable
(assuming that the wage paid by foreign firms is
greater than those by local firms). The removal of
the distortion in this case is a reduction in income
inequality, but the removal raises the reward of the
foreigners and therefore they stand to gain from
reduction in income inequalities. Moreover, its
removal need not raise welfare and therefore may
also be undesirable from an efficiency point of view.
Here is the dilemma for the policy maker efficiency
versus equity. Chapter 3 extends the framework of
this chapter to include a non-traded good and also
introduce partial mobility of foreign-owned capital.
Several results are again re-confirmed. This is
done in order to check the robustness of the results
already obtained. One result that needs special
mention is that class conflict (in the sense of

trade theorists, namely, in terms of demand for
protection) takes the form of a clash between
capitalists (both domestic and foreign) and workers.
A natural question to ask is: does the above
result regarding clash of interest hold in commonly
used trade models? The answer is in the negative.
In the framework of the Heckscher-Ohlin model with a
non-traded good and foreign ownership of capital in
the non-traded goods sector the demand for protection need not necessarily be a two class problem. It
is shown, among other things in Chapter 4, that in
terms of demand for protection labour and foreign
capitalists may agree to become strange 'bed
fellows'.
Chapter 5 casts serious doubts regarding the
frequently repeated theme that inflows of foreign
capital create employment. A counter example is
provided to show that an increase in the supply of
foreign-owned capital, in a minimum wage economy,
may not only increase unemployment but also lower
welfare.
Chapter 6 addresses itself to the problem of
indentured labour and its exploitation. The latter
term is defined in neoclassical terms as a payment
to the indentured workers below the value of their
marginal product. This difference in payment is
attributed to asymmetrical distribution of
information between buyers and sellers of labour. A
neoclassical exploitation function is set up and it
is shown that tasking increases the profits of the
foreign capitalists. Thus, tasking, exploitation
and generation of abnormal profits is not attributed
to racism - a theme commonly found in Fijian history.
Comments received from Professor W.M. Corden on
an initial draft of this book are gratefully
acknowledged. Two comments made by him require
special mention in the preface of this work. First,
Professor Corden regards the assumption of an
inelastic supply of foreign capital as grossly
unrealistic. This is an empirical question and
debatable. The inelastic supply of foreign capital
does capture the effects of monopoly power in trade
of capital - an area that is of interest in
discussions of unequal distribution of power. There
are two alternative assumptions regarding the shape
of supply curve of foreign capital. It may be
assumed that it is perfectly elastic - in this case
the rate of return gets determined from outside and
the quantity of capital flowing into the host
country endogenously. Most results of this book
would not follow under this particular assumption.

Alternatively it may be assumed that the supply curve of foreign capital is upward sloping but not completely inelastic. Under this assumption both the return on foreign capital and its quantity become endogenous variables. Obviously, in such a framework we cannot deal with issues relating to parametric shifts in the supply of capital in the sense in which the term is used in this book. However, such parametric changes can be captured by shifting the entire supply curve. I feel that several results obtained in this book will be re-confirmed in the above framework, but,of course, this cannot be stated with certainty. Second, Professor Corden raises the issue of taxation. The optimal tax is to retain all the earnings of foreign capital, i.e. the entire amount of repatriation payments so that the distinction between domestic and foreign capital vanishes. A similar sentiment has been expressed in a paper by Bhagwati and Brecher in the *Journal of Political Economy*, 1981, Vol.89.

Professor M.C. Kemp in private correspondence has written to me that the analysis in this book is "relentlessly static". He has suggested that the results be extended into a dynamic framework and should also include a discussion of exploitation of exhaustible resources. A most welcome suggestion which I hope to take up in a companion volume of this book.

Useful comments have also been received from Dr. R. Dubsky, Dr. H.M. Gunasekera, Dr. B. Lal, Dr. P.M. Sgro and Professor Eden Yu. I thank them all for the comments.

Unfortunately due to the hostility towards me of some (not all) Fiji Indians I was also denied the help of the editorial assistant of the School of Social and Economic Development to edit the manuscript. My friend and colleague at La Trobe, Mr. W. Horrigan, not only performed the above role admirably, but also provided me with comments of substance on the subject matter of the book. I am unable to express in suitable words my gratitude to him for the invaluable help he has given to me in preparation of this manuscript.

Most prefaces contain thanks to secretaries who toil along with the authors in preparing a manuscript for publication. This preface is no exception to the above rule but the history of employment of my secretary is noteworthy. In early 1981 my secretary left for Australia - a very competent Fiji Indian girl. Naturally, a new one

was required for the job. I was advised by well
meaning colleagues - "Bharat, be careful in hiring a
Fijian girl - they don't work as well as the Indians
do". Being new to the place I did not respond to
the above statement, but did hire the best
applicant which happened to be Ms. Taivuna Bulamaibau
- an exceptionally competent secretary. She has
performed her job magnificently; and moreover with
Bula smiles which are known all over the world.
Special thanks to Tai (as I came to address her) for
splendid secretarial help in truly Bula way!
        The responsibility for errors and omissions
rests with me.

                                Bharat R Hazari,
                                University of the South
                                    Pacific,
                                Suva, FIJI.

Chapter 1

COLONIALISM AND FOREIGN OWNERSHIP OF CAPITAL:

A TREATMENT IN A MODEL OF INTERNATIONAL TRADE

This chapter provides a framework for explaining
several themes that occur frequently in the
literature relating to economic development and
colonial economic history. Two of the themes often
developed are: (i) de-industrialization and
(ii) stagnation after an initial spurt in economic
activity. For example, in the context of Indian
economic history it is not clear whether there was a
process of de-industrialization, but there is no
doubt that several historians have made statements
about the "destruction" of the Indian handloom
industry. There are references to the "the ruin",
the "rapid collapse" and the almost "total
extinction" of this industry in the nineteenth
century.[1] One of the important objectives of this
chapter will be to show how the specificity of a
factor and its accumulation over time can result in
the decline of the traditional sector.
      In an important contribution Myint (13) made
the following remarks regarding stagnation after an
initial spurt in economic activity. He states, "The
transfer of labour from the subsistence economy to
the mines and plantations with their much higher
capital-output ratio and skilled management
undoubtedly resulted in a considerable increase in
productivity. But this was mostly of a once-for-all
character for a number of reasons".[2] We provide a
theoretical framework in which uncorrected monopoly
power in trade of capital can be seen to result in
stagnation of the type referred to by Myint.
      So far, our remarks have been confined to
themes that are often found in economic history. As
far as development in third world countries is
concerned, it is often asserted that the inflows of
foreign capital do not necessarily generate growth
and development. Several arguments are advanced

1

against the inflow of foreign capital (via multi-nationals, government and other aid agencies). For example, it is argued that these lower the domestic rate of saving and therefore act as substitutes for domestic capital.[3] It is also argued that foreign capital inflows create distortions which may be detrimental to the development process. Our model again provides a framework in which the inflow of foreign-owned capital does not generate development (except for its initial impact).

Having made these preliminary observations regarding the motivation for attempting the entire exercise, it is necessary to discuss some aspects of the structure of the model. The themes mentioned above are examined in terms of several positive and normative propositions which relate to the pure theory of international trade on the basis of a two-commodity, two-factor model in which foreign capital is assumed to be specific to one of the exportable sectors and available in inelastic supply.[4] The assumption that foreign capital is sector-specific may be justified on the basis of at least three arguments. First, foreign investors may have a preference for investing in only a few sectors of an underdeveloped economy. Second, in many developing countries foreign investors may be forbidden to invest in sectors considered to be of national and strategic importance. Finally, the model may be viewed as one which deals with a short-run situation in which capital (foreign-owned) is not mobile between the sectors in the economy. The assumption of an inelastic supply of foreign capital can be justified by two alternative, but not necessarily mutually exclusive arguments. First, as in the case of specificity, the model can be viewed as dealing with a short-run situation in which the stock of foreign-owned capital cannot be increased or decreased. Second, due to various types of government controls (for example, licensing) there may not exist a free flow of capital into a developing economy. Capital as a factor of production is much more mobile (though not perfectly mobile) as far as developed countries are concerned. The model can also be interpreted as one explaining some aspects of colonialism (which is defined as a situation where the country is governed by a foreign regime). The amount of capital brought into the colonies is determined by political considerations - a feature that is also present in today's third-world countries. The assumption of inelasticity of supply results in creating absolute monopoly power in trade

2

of capital for the metropolitan country.

1.1 The Model

In this section the two by-two-barter model of international trade is formally set up.

Let the utility function for the country as a whole be given by:

$$U = U(D_1, D_2) \tag{1.1}$$

where U indicates aggregate utility, and D_1, D_2 the domestic consumption of commodities 1 and 2. As usual, it is assumed that the function U is strictly concave and U_1 and U_2 are positive, where $U_i = \partial U/\partial D_i$. The results can also be derived by assuming quasi-concavity instead of strict concavity. The social utility function, U, is assumed to possess both behavioural and welfare significance.[5]

Utility maximization implies that at the point of equilibrium the ratio of the marginal utilities is equal to the commodity price ratio:

$$\frac{U_2}{U_1} = \frac{P_2}{P_1} = p \tag{1.2}$$

Further, it is assumed that both commodities are exported so that:

$$D_1 = X_1 - E_1 \tag{1.3}$$

$$D_2 = X_2 - E_2 \tag{1.4}$$

where X_i (i = 1,2) indicates the level of output and E_i (i = 1,2) represent the exports of commodities 1 and 2. It is, perhaps unusual to assume that both of the final goods are exported in exchange for the repatriation payments on foreign-owned capital. The model, however, can easily be extended to include a third good which is imported, but not produced domestically. This would be a more reasonable picture of a colonial economy.[6] The justification of not including the non-competitive imported final good is that its presence would not make any difference to the main results derived in this chapter; thus the presence of non-competitive imported final good can be ignored without any loss of generality. This is so because the presence of a non-competitive good will not enter the model from the production side.

3

The output of sector 1 is produced with the help of labour alone:

$$X_1 = F_1(L_1) \qquad (1.5)$$

It will be assumed that the marginal product of labour in this sector is strictly positive:

$$\frac{dX_1}{dL_1} > 0.$$

Furthermore, we shall also assume that:

$$\frac{d^2X_1}{dL_1^2} = 0$$

in other words, the marginal product of labour is constant. This assumption is relaxed in Chapter 2.

The production function for sector 2 predicates the use of two factors of production, labour and foreign-owned capital. The production function is assumed to exhibit constant returns to scale and diminishing returns along the isoquants. Hence the production function is:

$$X_2 = F_2(L_2, K_2^F) = L_2 f_2(k_2^F) \qquad (1.6)$$

where L_2 and K_2^F denote the allocation of labour and foreign capital to sector 2 and k_2^F the foreign capital-labour ratio in sector 2. Note that foreign capital is sector specific and is used in the production of the exportable commodity. This assumption is used here in order to relate this model to colonialism and also to adapt it at a later stage for dealing with the problem of "Girmit (indentured) labour" and its exploitation.

From the assumptions of profit maximization, incomplete specialisation and pure competition the following conditions regarding factor rewards can be derived:

$$w = \frac{dF_1}{dL_1} = p(f_2 - k_2^F f_2') \qquad (1.7)$$

$$r_F = pf_2 \qquad (1.8)$$

where w and r_F denote the real wage rate and the rental on foreign capital respectively. It is important to note here that, r_F, the rental on foreign capital, is fixed by domestic demand and supply considerations. The foreign investors accept a rate of return on their capital that is determined by the conditions in the host country. In the case of colonies and less-developed countries this rate is quite favourable due to shortages of capital.

There are two alternative assumptions in this context. First, that the rental on foreign capital is fixed exogenously and that the supply of foreign-owned capital is totally elastic. This would correspond to the small country assumption in the factor market. Second, it may be assumed that the supply of foreign capital is neither perfectly elastic nor perfectly inelastic-upward-sloping (non-vertical) supply curve of capital. In this case both the rate of return on foreign capital and the quantity of foreign capital brought into the host country are endogenously determined.[7] Both these assumptions appear to be unrealistic in colonial economies. They may also be unrealistic in several less-developed countries. This is so for reasons already spelled out in the introduction to this chapter.

The balance-of-payments equilibrium requires that the value of exports must equal the repatriation payments on foreign capital. Hence:

$$E_1 + pE_2 = r_F \bar{K}^F \tag{1.9}$$

It is assumed that resources are fully employed so that:

$$L_1 + L_2 = \bar{L} \tag{1.10}$$

$$k_2^F L_2 = \bar{K}^F \tag{1.11}$$

where $\bar{L}$ and $\bar{K}^F$ denote the inelastically supplied total amounts of labour and foreign capital. The model is closed by assuming that the country is small and takes the prices of final commodities as given, i.e. p.

It should be pointed out that the assumption of an endogenously determined return on foreign capital leads to the emergence of a market imperfection - specifically monopoly power in trade of capital. Obviously the correct policy is an optimum tax on the return to foreign capital. However, this may

5

not be imposed for two different reasons. First, in a colonial economy the government would not be interested in taxing its own gains from the presence of the above monopoly power. Second, in the case of third world countries such a tax may not be imposed at the optimal level because it is feared that it may jeopardise future inflows of foreign capital which are regarded as beneficial for the host country. [8] It will be assumed that repatriation payments are untaxed and the consequences of the presence of monopoly power examined. A number of new and interesting results are presented in the following sections.

1.2 Output-Endowment Theorems and Welfare

The model presented above consists of two factors: (i) a mobile factor labour and (ii) a specific factor foreign capital. The implications of foreign capital accumulation are examined first. To obtain the output effect of foreign capital accumulation the production functions are differentiated at constant commodity prices:

$$\frac{dX_1}{d\bar{K}^F} = \frac{dF_1}{dL_1} \frac{dL_1}{d\bar{K}^F} \tag{1.12}$$

$$\frac{dX_2}{d\bar{K}^F} = f_2 \frac{dL_2}{d\bar{K}^F} \tag{1.13}$$

Note that at constant prices the foreign capital-labour ratio cannot change and therefore the output response depends only on re-allocation of labour and absorption of foreign capital. The explicit solutions for $dL_i/d\bar{K}^F$, (i = 1,2) can be obtained from the factor-endowment equations. By using these expressions the following output responses are obtained:

$$\frac{dX_1}{d\bar{K}^F} = - \frac{w}{k_2^F} \tag{1.14}$$

$$\frac{dX_2}{d\bar{K}^F} = \frac{f_2}{k_2^F} \tag{1.15}$$

It is obvious from equations (1.14) and (1.15) that

6

the output of sector 1, the traditional sector
declines absolutely, and the output of sector 2
which uses foreign capital expands absolutely when
foreign capital accumulation occurs. Before
commenting on this very interesting result it is
worth looking at the situation in geometrical
terms.[9]
    Given the assumption of inelastic supply of
factors of production a box diagram can be constructed to portray the foreign capital and labour endowments of the economy. In Figure 1.1 the vertical
line O_2A measures the amount of foreign capital
available and O_1A (which equals O_2B) the total
supply of labour. Since it has been assumed that
foreign capital is sector-specific production must
occur on the line AO_1. The output of sector 2 is
measured from the origin O_2 and labour allocation to
sector 1 from origin O_1. Suppose the initial
equilibrium occurs at point E which is shown by the
tangency between the isoquant of sector 2, x_2x_2 and
the factor price ratio given by the slope of the
line CD. Sector 2 uses O_2A of foreign capital (the
total amount available) and AE amount of labour.
The output of sector 1 is a function of labour only.
Sector 1 uses the remaining amount of labour, namely,
O_1E. Let the stock of the foreign capital increase
from O_2A to O_2A'. At constant prices and therefore
at constant factor intensity the new equilibrium now
occurs at point E' where the isoquant $x_2'x_2'$ is
tangential to the factor price ratio C'D'. Clearly
the output of sector 2 has increased. From the
diagram it is also clear that the amount of labour
available to sector   1 has declined from O_1E to
$O_1'E'$. Since the output of sector 1 is a function of
labour only, it must also decline.
    Two observations need to be made regarding the
above result. First, on account of specificity of
one of the factors the output movements do not
depend upon factor intensities. Hence in the two
sector model presented here the output-endowment
result is different from the Rybczynski theorem.
This result may be viewed as the limiting case of
the Rybczynski theorem where one sector is so
capital-intensive relative to the other that no
capital at all is used in the traditional sector.
While this is true it should be clearly noted that
with specificity capital intensities do not play any
role in the qualitative nature of results (in the
present framework). In fact this possibility is
logically ruled out of consideration in the model.
The sector using the specific factor expands and the

Figure 1.1

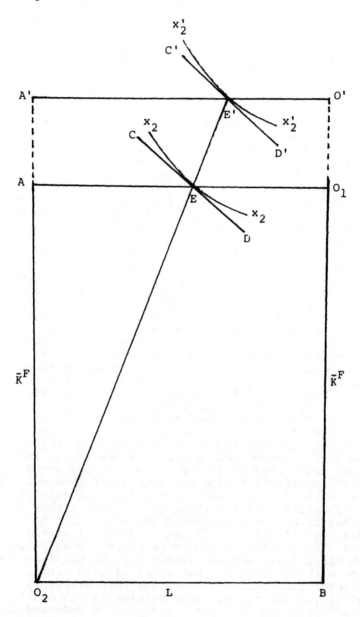

8

sector not using the specific factor contracts (given fixed commodity prices). Second, given the assumption that the specific factor is foreign-capital the model provides an interesting result for explaining de-industrialization in colonial economies. If we interpret X_1 to be the traditional sector then the results show that successive doses of foreign capital (colonial investments) would lead to successive contractions in the output of the traditional sector. In the limit the traditional sector will go out of existence. Note that this result requires the assumption of a small open economy so that the commodity prices can be held constant. De-industrialization occurs due to factor specificity combined with the assumption of a small economy and not on account of deliberate economic policy which might cause the decline of the traditional sector. This is not to say that such policies have not been pursued in colonial history: it is simply meant to emphasise the role of factor specificity and smallness in the destruction of traditional sectors.[10]

The analysis now turns to an examination of the welfare implications of foreign capital accumulation. By differentiating the utility function (equation (1.1)) with respect to foreign-owned capital the following expression is obtained:

$$\frac{1}{U_1} \frac{dU}{d\bar{K}^F} = \frac{dD_1}{d\bar{K}^F} + p \frac{dD_2}{d\bar{K}^F} \qquad (1.16)$$

This equation can be simplified with the help of equations (1.13), (1.14), (1.9), (1.16) and (1.17) to yield:

$$\frac{1}{U_1} \frac{dU}{d\bar{K}^F} = 0 \qquad (1.17)$$

Equation (1.17) shows that an increase in the stock of foreign capital does not alter the welfare level of the colony or host country. The explanation of this result is quite simple. Recall that both factors receive the value of their marginal product. An increase in foreign capital raises income precisely by the value of marginal product of foreign capital, but this income goes out of the country as repatriation payments leaving welfare of the host country or colony completely unchanged.

An obvious question in the above context is: does the inflow of foreign capital help the receiving country at all in this framework? The answer depends on whether trade occurs or not. In an autarky position, the economy is only capable of producing commodity X_1. Therefore the equilibrium solution occurs at a corner point in the output space. This is illustrated in Figure 1.2a. The economy is not capable of producing commodity X_2 without foreign capital. Therefore the transformation curve for the closed economy consists of the vertical distance $O\bar{X}_1$. The point $\bar{X}_1$ is associated with full employment of the labour force, i.e. $\bar{X}_1 = F_1(\bar{L})$. Assuming full employment equilibrium occurs at point $\bar{X}_1$, then the autarky welfare is shown by the indifference curve U_a. Note that in the closed economy X_1 is a non-traded good.

The inflow of foreign capital either in the modern setting or a colonial regime undoubtedly leads to diversification of the production structure by making the production of X_2 feasible. Therefore, the production transformation curve acquires its more normal shape $\bar{X}_1\bar{X}_2$ in Figure 1.2b where $\bar{X}_2$ is the maximum output of X_2 that can be generated when all factors are employed by sector 2, i.e. $\bar{X}_2 = F_2$ $(\bar{L}, \bar{K}^F)$. It should be pointed out that consumption cannot occur on the locus $\bar{X}_1\bar{X}_2$. From this locus the repatriation payments on foreign capital (equal to the value of exports) must be subtracted. After this adjustment one obtains the net locus. This net locus is shown as X_1T_2 in Figures 1.3a and 1.3b.

We now examine the ranking in welfare terms of a closed economy (in which $\bar{X}_1 = D_1$) with an open economy which receives foreign capital (either through a colonial regime or in a more modern setting). Two scenarios can be postulated in this situation. In one case although foreign capital is capable of expanding the production transformation locus no trade occurs due to the curvature of the social indifference curve. Obviously no comparison can be made between the autarky and a trading position as shown in Figure 1.3a.[11] However, if trade occurs, then the inflow of foreign capital not only diversifies production but also raises welfare as shown in Figure 1.3b. Autarky consumption and production equilibrium is indicated by point $\bar{X}_1$ and welfare level by U_a. The inflow of foreign capital results in equilibrium at point C_F and welfare level U_F. It is obvious that $U_F > U_a$ therefore the level of welfare increases. Note that point C_F is a position of trading equilibrium. This is so because both goods are exported in exchange for repatriation payments made to foreign owners of capital. This

Figure 1.2a

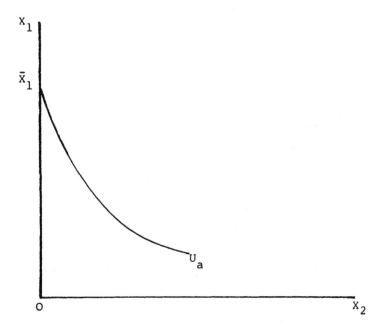

Figure 1.2b

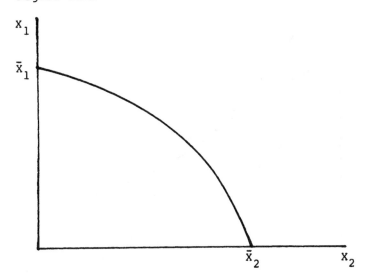

Figure 1.3a

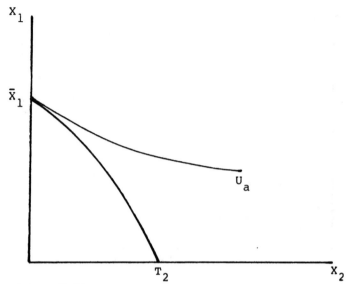

Figure 1.3b

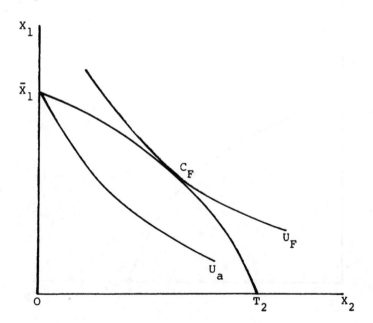

adjustment has already been made in deriving the net production possibility locus $\bar{X}_1 T_2$. It is obvious from Figure 1.3b that national income increases when trade occurs. Note that labour is the only domestic factor and an increase in national income must raise the wage rate in the economy. Thus the wage rate in the trading economy is higher than in autarky.

The reader may feel a bit confused by the above result because of the assumption of a constant marginal product in the traditional sector. The result can be explained intuitively in the following manner. In the closed economy only X_1 is produced and consumed and therefore there is no relative price. The metropolitan country, by bringing foreign capital into the host country, makes the production of X_2 feasible and also introduces a relative price ratio. This price ratio is such that it raises the real wage rate in the economy. This is possible, for example, by the introduction of a relatively cheaper new product, namely X_2. The introduction of a cheaper new product raises the real wage, which of course, raises welfare. This result can also be derived by assuming diminishing returns in the traditional sector.

A few interesting observations may be made in the context of a model of colonialism. First, the initial inflow of foreign capital results in an expansion of production activities and raises welfare. More importantly every successive inflow leaves the welfare level unchanged. In other words, after the initial round of activity foreign capital makes no contribution whatsoever to the welfare of the colonial economy.[12] Second, on account of specificity of foreign capital and fixed prices successive inflows of foreign capital lead to a decline of the traditional sector. Both these results have been noted in economic history, but to my knowledge they have not been explained in terms of factor specificity and payment to foreign capital based on its marginal product in the host country (colony)(which in our model gives absolute monopoly power to the metropolitan country).

We now consider the implications of accumulation of the domestic factor labour, at fixed commodity prices. By following the procedures already outlined it follows that:

$$\frac{dX_1}{d\bar{L}} = \frac{dF_1}{dL_1} = w \tag{1.18}$$

13

$$\frac{dX_2}{d\bar{L}} = 0 \qquad\qquad (1.19)$$

Thus the output of the traditional sector expands
and that of the sector using foreign capital remains
unchanged. The explanation of this result follows
from the assumption of fixed commodity prices. At
constant prices it is known that k_2^F, the foreign
capital intensity cannot change, therefore it
follows from the factor endowment condition that the
allocation of labour to sector 2 cannot change.
Since the output of sector 2 depends on labour
allocation and foreign capital intensity (which
remain constant), it follows that the output of
sector 2 must remain constant which is exactly the
result shown in equation (1.19). The above result
can be portrayed geometrically by utilising the
technique used in Figure 1.1.

Let us now consider the implications for
welfare of the growth in the domestic factor labour.
By following the procedure outlined earlier we
arrive at the following expression:

$$\frac{1}{U_1} \frac{dU}{d\bar{L}} = w > 0 \qquad\qquad (1.20)$$

Obviously welfare increases with the accumulation of
the domestically-owned factor.

The contrast between foreign and domestic
factor accumulation is quite interesting. First,
the accumulation of foreign-owned factor contributes
nothing to the domestic economy (except for its
initial impact) whereas the accumulation of the
domestic factor always raises welfare, in spite of
the presence of monopoly power in trade of capital
(distortion).[13] Second, the growth of the sector
using foreign-owned capital always leads to a
contraction of the traditional sector whereas the
increase in the supply of domestic factor leaves the
sector using foreign capital completely unchanged.
This brings to end our discussion of the effects of
factor accumulation on output levels and welfare.

1.3 An Increase in the Price of the Exportable
Good Using Foreign Capital and Welfare

The implication of an increase in the price of the
exportable good using foreign-owned capital for
welfare can now be considered. By differentiating

the utility function (1.1) with respect to p we
obtain:

$$\frac{1}{U_1} \frac{dU}{dp} = \frac{dD_1}{dp} + p \frac{dD_2}{dp} \qquad (1.21)$$

By differentiating equations (1.3), (1.4) and (1.9)
it follows:

$$\frac{dD_1}{dp} = \frac{dX_1}{dp} - \frac{dE_1}{dp} \qquad (1.22)$$

$$\frac{dD_2}{dp} = \frac{dX_2}{dp} - \frac{dE_2}{dp} \qquad (1.23)$$

$$\frac{dE_1}{dp} + \frac{dE_2}{dp} = \bar{K}^F \frac{dr_F}{dp} - E_2 \qquad (1.24)$$

By utilising equations (1.22), (1.23) and (1.24) the
expression in equation (1.21) can be simplified to:

$$\frac{1}{U_1} \frac{dU}{dp} = E_2 - \bar{K}^F \frac{dr_F}{dp} \qquad (1.25)$$

The above equation can be simplified further. First,
the expression for dr_F/dp is obtained by differentiating equation (1.8) with respect to p. By
suitable manipulation it follows:

$$\frac{dr_F}{dp} = \frac{f_2}{k_2^F} \qquad (1.26)$$

Note that the above expression is always positive;
in other words the return to foreign capital always
increases as a consequence of an increase in the
price of the commodity in whose production foreign
capital is used. The above expression has been
derived on the assumption that the marginal product
of labour is constant in sector 1 - an assumption
that is relaxed in the next chapter.
From equation (1.4) it is clear that:

$$E_2 = X_2 - D_2 = L_2 f_2 - D_2 \qquad (1.27)$$

By using equations (1.27) and (1.26) equation (1.25)
can be written as:

15

$$\frac{1}{U_1} \frac{dU}{dp} = - D_2 \qquad (1.28)$$

Expression (1.28) clearly shows that an increase in the price of the exportable good which uses foreign capital always lowers national welfare. This result is independent of having an importable sector in the model.

This is a most fascinating result, evoking a number of comments. The intuitive explanation of the above result is given below. In order to appreciate the reasons underlying the result contained in equation (1.28) the approach of Jones (11) to rewrite factor price equations can be utilised. These can be written as:

$$a_{L1}w = 1 \qquad (1.29)$$

$$a_{L2}w + a_{KF}r_F = p \qquad (1.30)$$

where a_{ij}s denote input coefficients. The labour input coefficient in sector 1 has been assumed to be a constant. By differentiating equation (1.29) with respect to p it is clear that:

$$\frac{dw}{dp} = 0 \qquad (1.31)$$

By using and differentiating equation (1.30) it follows:

$$\Theta_{KF}\hat{r}_F = \hat{p} \qquad (1.32)$$

where Θ_{KF} is the share of capital in sector 2, $\hat{r}_F = dr_F/r_F$ and $\hat{p} = dp/p$. Since Θ_{KF} is less than unity ($\Theta_{KF} < 1$) it follows that:

$$\hat{r}_F > \hat{p} \qquad (1.33)$$

In other words the rental on foreign capital rises more than the price ratio. Recall that both commodities are exported and that foreign capital is imported. Therefore by virtue of equation (1.33) an increase in the relative price of the sector using foreign capital results in a deterioration in the terms of trade because of the variation in rental on foreign capital. Hence, it is not surprising that welfare of the host (colonial) country declines as a result of an increase in the price of exports.

The above result is a direct consequence of uncorrected monopoly power in trade of capital. In the absence of such monopoly power the rental on foreign capital would be given exogenously and foreign capital would be in perfectly elastic supply. In such a situation the expression relating to dr_F/dp in equation (1.32) would equal zero and the deterioration in terms of trade would in fact become an improvement in terms of trade. It should be pointed out that the above result may also follow (but not in such a strong form) if the repatriation payments are partially taxed. Only in the case of a 100% tax on repatriation payments would the results be identical to those obtained in the first best framework. Of course even partial taxation was absent in colonial times and 100% tax is absent in modern times. Therefore, the impact of an increase in the price of exportable good does not have an unambigous effect on the welfare of the host country.

1.4 Conclusions

It is now possible to summarise the results derived from a simple model of colonialism (broadly interpreted as a model of foreign ownership of factors of production in a third world situation). The model presented is one in which there are two sectors, one which uses domestic factors of production and the other that uses domestic and foreign factors of production. The supply of foreign capital is exogenously determined (for example, by political considerations). The important results presented are given below. First, concerning results related to economic expansion, output movements and welfare, the model shows that economic expansion, in the partially foreign-owned sector does not lead to an improvement in the welfare of the host country - a result that occurs thanks to the presence of monopoly power in trade of capital. Obviously a colonial regime would not be interested in correcting the presence of such monopoly power. Moreover, expansion of the modern sector leads to a decline in the output of the traditional sector and in the limit the output of the traditional sector falls to zero. Thus, de-industrialization in a small open economy is shown to occur because of specificity of foreign-owned capital and fixed commodity prices - no other assumptions (for instance, racism) are needed to explain de-industrialization. Finally, economic expansion of the domestically-owned sector always raises welfare. Thus growth in such a

17

framework only occurs on the basis of indigenous factors or causes. This is a result which provides some rationale for the current discussion in literature on third world countries which asserts that development occurs through domestic factors only. An interesting result in this context is that the growth of domestic factors does not affect the size of the sector using foreign-owned capital. Finally it should be added that the presence of monopoly power in trade of capital leads to the rather surprising result that every increase in the relative price of an exportable good that uses foreign capital lowers welfare. This results in the inability of the country to take advantage of favourable movements in the price of one of the exportable commodities.

NOTES

1. These statements are from Chandra (2).
2. See Myint (13),p.321.
3. See for example Hazari (7) and Weisskopf (16).
4. A more general version of this type of model has been explored by Hazari and Pattanaik (8) and in Chapter 2.
5. Note that this is a utility function that ignores externalities. For example in the context of foreign-owned capital one may be inclined to argue that its (foreign capital) presence generates a feeling of hate and depression in the minds of several people in less-developed countries. Obviously in such a case the presence of foreign-owned capital lowers their welfare. Such problems although present are outside the framework of this chapter. Remember that we have an aggregate utility function - which is beset with the usual problems of aggregation. If some people like the presence of foreign capital and others do not, then the utility functions across individuals are not identical and therefore in such a situation it would not be possible to come up with a well behaved aggregate utility function.
6. This is not an unreasonable assumption in a historical context. Raychaudhuri (14) makes the following statement about India, "Except for an insignificant amount of luxury goods, like richly carved swords, and occasionally, cannon, India imported no manufactured metal products before the nineteenth century".
7. This assumption has been used, for example by Corden (3).

8. Obviously this is a simplifying assumption. Most countries now impose a corporate income tax. This tax can be imposed in this model. In order to achieve this the balance-of-payments and the factor reward conditions need to be suitably adjusted.
9. Note that this result does not depend on whether repatriation payments are taxed or not and also different from Rybczynski Theorem. This result is also a subset of results obtained by Hazari (5) and Fishburn and Kemp (4).
10. This result obviously sheds some light on the statement quoted earlier from Chandra (2).
11. A similar result has been noted in the context of non-traded goods by Hazari-Sgro-Suh (10) p.21.
12. Uncorrected monopoly power provides another perspective regarding the statements made by Myint (13) in his well-known paper (quoted earlier in the opening remarks in this chapter). This type of monopoly power has also remained uncorrected in history. The following statement of Raychaudhuri (14) is quite illuminating, "the public demand for state action to protect the Indian industries going back to the eighties of the nineteenth century, the swadeshi movement which came about a quarter of a century later, the idiolisation of the new 'heroes' of industry - all these indicate that the tension Gerschenkron speaks of as also in ideology of indus-trialization were not lacking the late nineteenth century India. Only the appropriate policies which the situation called for did not emerge. The state followed a laissez-fare policy not out of any line of doctrines, but because the relevant decisions were ultimately determined by the interests of the British economy, British private capital in particular", p.97.
13. This is possible in the presence of distortions, see the papers by Hazari and Pattanaik (8) and Hazari and Sgro (9).

REFERENCES

(1) Bhattachrya, S. 1965. Laissez-fare in India. *Indian Economic and Social History Review*, Vol.2, (January) 1-22.
(2) Chandra, B. 1966. *The Rise and Growth of Economic Nationalism in India*. New Delhi: Peoples Publishing House.
(3) Corden, W.M. 1974. *Trade Policy and Economic Welfare*. London: Oxford University Press.

(4) Fishburn, G. and Kemp, M.C. 1977. An Analysis
of Price: Rental and Endowment: Output Relationships in Terms of Specific Factors and Product
Blocks. *Economic Record*, Vol.53 (June-September)
219-26.
(5) Hazari, B.R. 1977. Factor Accumulation, Terms of
Trade and Welfare in a Three Commodity, Three
Factor Model of International Trade. *Australian
Economic Papers*, Vol.17 (December) 267-72.
(6) ———— 1978. *The Pure Theory of International
Trade and Distortions*. London: Croom Helm.
(7) ———— 1980. *The Structure of the Indian Economy:
An Analysis*. New Delhi: Macmillan and Company.
(8) Hazari, B.R. and Pattanaik, P.K. 1980. Some
Welfare Propositions in a Three Commodity, Three
Factor Model of Trade in the Presence of Foreign-
Owned Factors of Production. *Greek Economic
Review*, Vol.2 (April) 12-33.
(9) Hazari, B.R. and Sgro, P.M. 1980. Theorems on
Immiserising Growth (Normal Growth) in the Non-
Traded Goods and Wage Differential Framework: An
Extension. *Southern Economic Journal*, Vol.47
(July), 241-43.
(10) Hazari, B.R., Sgro, P.M. and Suh, D.C. 1981.
*Non-Traded and Intermediate Goods and the Pure
Theory of International Trade*. London: Croom
Helm.
(11) Jones, R.W. 1965. The Structure of Simple
General Equilibrium Models. *Journal of Political
Economy*, Vol.73 (December) 557-72.
(12) Lamb, H. 1955. The 'State' and Economic
Development in India. In S. Kuznets *et al* (ed.),
Economic Growth: Brazil, India and Japan. Durham:
Duke University Press.
(13) Myint, H. 1958. The Gains from International
Trade and the Backward Countries. In A.M. Agara-
wala and S.P. Singh (ed.), *The Economics of
Underdevelopment*. Bombay: Oxford University Press.
(14) Raychaudhuri, T. 1969. A Reinterpretation of
Nineteenth Century Indian Economic History. In
Morris D. Morris ed. (*et al*), *Indian Economy in
the Nineteenth Century: A Symposium*. Delhi:
Hindustan Publishing Corporation.
(15) Rybczynski, T.M. 1955. Factor Endowments and
Relative Commodity Prices. *Economica*, Vol.22
(November), 181-97.
(16) Weisskopf, T.E. 1972. The Impact of Foreign
Capital Inflow on Domestic Savings in Under-
developed Countries. *Journal of International
Economics*, Vol.2 (February) 25-38.

Chapter 2

SOME WELFARE PROPOSITIONS IN A THREE COMMODITY,

THREE FACTOR MODEL OF INTERNATIONAL TRADE IN

THE PRESENCE OF FOREIGN OWNED CAPITAL[1]

The object of this chapter is to generalise the
framework already developed. Recall that the model
of Chapter 1 had two sectors both of which produced
exportable commodities. There was no importable
sector. Two factors of production were used in the
production of the commodities, domestically-supplied
labour and sector specific foreign capital.

This framework can now be extended to introduce
a third sector: an importable sector which produces
commodity X_3. One more primary factor of production
is also introduced: domestic capital which is used
in the production of sectors 1 and 3. Thus, the
output of sector 1 now depends on domestic labour
and domestic capital (similarly for sector 3).

The extended model consists of three commodities
and three factors, one of the factors is assumed to
be specific to one of the sectors. There are at
least three real life situations which can be
conveniently represented by this type of model.
First, consider a country like Australia in which two
types of agricultural goods are produced with the
help of land and labour while a manufactured good is
produced with the help of labour and capital.
Alternatively, consider an economy in which two
commodities may be produced with the help of capital
and labour while the third commodity is produced with
the help of capital and highly skilled imported
labour. Lastly, one can take the case of a developing country (or a colony) in which two sectors
produce their output with the help of labour and
domestic capital, while the third sector uses labour
and foreign capital. In all the three cases one
factor is specific to a sector, one factor is
completely mobile among all the sectors and one
factor is mobile between only two sectors. It is
proposed to concentrate on the last case only (where

the specific factor is assumed to be foreign capital). The other versions can easily be analysed in the framework developed for the case examined by making suitable adjustments to the balance-of-payments equation and by reinterpreting the production relationships.

In contrast to the previous model it will now also be assumed that the inflow of foreign capital results in creating a domestic distortion - specifically a wage differential.[2] Thus, this model will be characterised by two distortions:(i) monopoly power in trade due to inelastic supply of foreign capital and (ii) a distortionary wage differential.[3] The distortions will invariably be defined from the source.[4]

2.1 The Model

In this section the three-by-three barter model of international trade is formally set up.

Let the utility function for the country as a whole be given by:

$$U = U(D_1, D_2, D_3) \qquad (2.1)$$

where U indicates utility, and D_1, D_2, D_3, indicate the domestic consumption of commodities 1, 2 and 3 respectively. As usual, it is assumed that U is strictly concave and U_1, U_2, and U_3 are all positive (where $U_i = \partial U / \partial D_i$, $i = 1...3$).

At an interior point of utility maximization it is known that the following condition is satisfied:

$$\frac{U_1}{p_1} = \frac{U_2}{p_2} = \frac{U_3}{p_3} \qquad (2.2)$$

where $p_i (i = 1...3)$ indicates the prices of commodities 1, 2 and 3.

It is assumed that parts of domestic production of commodities 1 and 2 are exported and a part of the domestic consumption of commodity 3 is imported, so that:

$$D_1 = X_1 - E_1 \qquad (2.3)$$

$$D_2 = X_2 - E_2 \qquad (2.4)$$

$$D_3 = X_3 + M_3 \qquad (2.5)$$

22

where $X_i (i = 1 ... 3)$ indicates the level of output, $E_i (i = 1, 2)$ represents exports, and M_3, imports of good 3.

The balance-of-payments equilibrium requires that the value of exports must equal the sum of value of imports and repatriation of rental on foreign capital. Hence:

$$p_1 E_1 + p_2 E_2 = p_3 M_3 + r_F \bar{K}^F \qquad (2.6)$$

where r_F indicates the rental on foreign capital and $r_F \bar{K}^F$ the value of repatriation payments.

It is assumed that the production function for the three commodities exhibit constant returns to scale and diminishing returns along the isoquants. Note that the assumption of constant marginal product in sector 1 has been relaxed (an assumption that was made in Chapter 1). Hence, the production functions are:

$$X_1 = F_1 (L_1, K_1^d) = L_1 f_1 (k_1^d) \qquad (2.7)$$

$$X_2 = F_2 (L_2, K_2^F) = L_2 f_2 (k_2^F) \qquad (2.8)$$

$$X_3 = F_3 (L_3, K_3^d) = L_3 f_3 (k_3^d) \qquad (2.9)$$

where $L_i (i = 1 ... 3)$, $K_i^d (i = 1, 3)$ and K_2^F denote the labour domestic capital and foreign capital allocation to the ith sector, while $k_i^d (i = 1, 3)$ and k_2^F the domestic and foreign capital intensity. Note that there are three factors of production which are characterised by different mobilities: labour is assumed to be completely mobile between sectors, domestic capital mobile between sectors 1 and 3, and foreign capital which is assumed to be specific to sector 2.

The distortionary wage differential is introduced in the following form:

$$w = \alpha w_2 \qquad \alpha \neq 1 \text{ and } \qquad \alpha > 0 \qquad (2.10)$$

where w indicates the wage rate in sectors 1 and 3 and w_2 the wage in sector 2.

From the assumptions of profit maximization, incomplete specialisation and perfect competition the following conditions regarding factor rewards can be derived:

23

$$w = p_1(f_1 - k_1^d f_1') = \alpha p_2(f_2 - k_2^F f_2') = p_3(f_3 - k_3^d f_3') \qquad (2.11)$$

$$\pi = p_1 f_1' = p_3 f_3' \qquad (2.12)$$

$$r_F = p_2 f_2' \qquad (2.13)$$

where π denotes the rental on domestic capital.
It is assumed that resources are fully employed, so that:

$$k_1^d L_1 + k_3^d L_3 = \bar{K}^d \qquad (2.14)$$

$$L_1 + L_2 + L_3 = \bar{L} \qquad (2.15)$$

$$k_2^F L_2 = \bar{K}^F \qquad (2.16)$$

Equations (2.1) to (2.16) represent a more complex model than that presented in the preceding chapter.

2.2 Changes in the Degree of Distortion and Welfare

The above model can now be utilised to examine the impact of reduction in the degree of distortion, specifically wage differential (at constant commodity prices), on welfare. First the formal results will be derived and then follow some comments, not only on their significance, but also on the desire to reduce the degree of distortion. By differentiating equations (2.1), (2.2), (2.3), (2.4), (2.5), (2.6) with respect to α and suitable arrangement of terms, the following equation is obtained:

$$\frac{1}{U_1}\frac{dU}{d\alpha} = \frac{dX_1}{d\alpha} + \frac{p_2}{p_1}\frac{dX_2}{d\alpha} + \frac{p_3}{p_1}\frac{dX_3}{d\alpha} - \frac{\bar{K}^F}{p_1}\frac{dr_F}{d\alpha} \qquad (2.17)$$

The solutions for $dX_i/d\alpha$ ($i = 1...3$) and $dr_F/d\alpha$ can be obtained by using equations (2.7), (2.8), (2.9), (2.11), (2.12), (2.13), (2.14), (2.15) and (2.16). These solutions are given below:

$$\frac{dX_1}{d\alpha} = -\frac{f_1 L_2 k_3^d}{k_2^F(k_1^d - k_3^d)}\frac{dk_2^F}{d\alpha} \qquad (2.18)$$

$$\frac{dX_2}{d\alpha} = -\frac{L_2(f_2 - k_2^F f_2')}{k_2^F}\frac{dk_2^F}{d\alpha} \tag{2.19}$$

$$\frac{dX_3}{d\alpha} = \frac{k_1^d L_2 f_3}{k_2^F(k_1^d - k_3^d)}\frac{dk_2^F}{d\alpha} \tag{2.20}$$

$$\frac{dk_2^F}{d\alpha} = \frac{(f_2 - k_2^F f_2')}{\alpha k_2^F f_2''} < 0 \tag{2.21}$$

$$\frac{dr_F}{d\alpha} = \frac{w}{\alpha^2 k_2^F} > 0 \tag{2.22}$$

By using equations (2.18) to (2.22) equation (2.17) can be simplified to:

$$\frac{1}{U_1}\frac{dU}{d\alpha} = A(\alpha-1)w_2 - \bar{K}^F\frac{p_2}{p_1}f_2''\frac{dk_2^F}{d\alpha} \tag{2.23}$$

where $A = \dfrac{L_2}{k_2^F}\dfrac{dk_2^F}{d\alpha}$.

On the basis of the above equations several interesting results emerge.

Proposition 2.1: A reduction in the degree of distortion (in the wage differential) raises (lowers) the return to foreign capital (equation 2.22) depending on $\alpha < 1$ ($\alpha > 1$).

Consider the realistic case of $\alpha < 1$. This assumption implies that the wages of workers working in sector 2 (foreign capital using sector) are higher than workers who work in the totally domestically-owned sector. It is often apparent in less-developed countries that many firms which use foreign capital as a specific factor pay a reward greater than that paid by firms producing with locally supplied inputs. Proposition 2.1 highlights that any reduction (i.e for $\alpha < 1$) always raises the return on foreign capital. Therefore, contrary to popular belief a reduction in wage differential (for $\alpha < 1$) inevitably helps the owners of foreign capital. This is a rather disturbing result for policy makers - a reduction in distortions, a desirable social

25

objective in third world countries, results in gains for foreign-owned factor of production.

Now consider the interrelationship between the degree of distortion and welfare. This can be analysed on the basis of equation (2.23). It is obvious that:

$$\frac{dk_2^F}{d\alpha} < 0.$$

Hence, the second term in equation (2.23) is always negative. The sign of the first term may be positive or negative, depending on α (A is always negative). If $\alpha > 1$ then the first term is negative, hence, a reduction in the degree of distortion always raises welfare. On the other hand if $\alpha < 1$ then the first term in equation (2.23) is positive, while the second term is negative. Hence, for $\alpha < 1$ the effect of a reduction in the degree of distortion is ambiguous.

Proposition 2.2: If $\alpha > 1$, then an increase (decrease) in the degree of wage differential always reduces (increases) welfare.

Proposition 2.3: If $\alpha < 1$, then a decrease in the degree of wage differential lowers welfare if and only if the following inequality is satisfied:

$$A(\alpha-1)w_2 - \bar{K}^F \frac{P_2}{P_1} f''_2 \frac{dk_2^F}{d\alpha} < 0 \qquad (2.24)$$

The intuitive explanation of the above results can easily be developed. We only offer an explanation for Proposition 2.3. The value of $\alpha < 1$ implies that $w_2 > w$, in other words the wage rate in sector 2 (the sector using foreign capital as a specific factor) is higher than in the other two sectors. Now suppose that the degree of wage differential is reduced. This reduction affects welfare through two terms in equation (2.23), one term capturing the productivity gain or loss (the first term) and the other term the effect of repatriation payments. Now from equations (2.19) and (2.22) we know that:

$$\frac{dx_2}{d\alpha} > 0$$

and

$$\frac{dr_F}{d\alpha} > 0.$$

Hence, with a reduction in the wage differential (which implies a rise in α because $\alpha < 1$), the foreign repatriation payments always increase, which imposes a burden on the economy. The first term in the present case represents a gain to the economy because $w_2 > w$ and labour moves from low productivity sectors to high productivity sectors on account of reduction in the degree of distortion. The total outcome depends on the magnitude of these two effects, one representing a loss and the other a gain. In the case covered by Proposition 2.3, the loss dominates the gain.

It has already been remarked that $\alpha < 1$ is realistic in the context of less-developed countries and colonial economies. Many firms which use foreign capital as specific factor pay a reward greater than that paid by firms producing with locally supplied inputs.[6] The result seen above creates a dilemma for the policy makers. On equity grounds, governments would prefer to reduce wage differentials, although as we have seen, such reductions are not necessarily desirable from a welfare point of view. Thus, Proposition 2.3 highlights the conflict between equity and welfare in a neo-classical model of international trade.

Proposition 2.3 is related to a result proved by Batra and Pattanaik (1). On the basis of the traditional two-by-two barter model of trade, Batra and Pattanaik show that an increased differential may increase welfare if value intensity reversals occur. Proposition 2.3 demonstrates that such an outcome is also possible outside the Heckscher-Ohlin framework.

At first sight, the Batra-Pattanaik result as well as Proposition 2.3 may seem to contradict the following theorem of Bhagwati(3): "Reductions in the degree of (an only) distortion are successively welfare increasing until distortion is fully eliminated". In fact Batra and Pattanaik (and also Magee (13) at a later date) claimed that their result constituted a counter-example to Bhagwati's theorem. However, this assertion of Batra and Pattanaik and Magee is erroneous. For Bhagwati's theorem applies to cases where only one distortion exists in the system and, in terms of his definition a constant wage differential leads to two distortions:

(a) Domestic Marginal Rate of Transformation $\neq$
    Domestic Marginal Rate of Substitution =
    Marginal Rate of Transformation; and

(b) Operation inside the production possibility
    frontier.[7]

Bhagwati defines four principal types of distortions (three in terms of inequalities in the rates of transformation and the fourth as a shrinkage of the production possibility locus). Thus, the number of distortions is determined not in terms of their intuitive sources but in terms of their consequences. Given this definition of Bhagwati, neither the Batra-Pattanaik result nor Proposition 2.3 contradicts Bhagwati's theorem. It should also be stated that Bhagwati's theorem could be seen as a tautology. This is so because distoritons are defined in terms of consequences. If there is only one distortion in terms of consequences, then its increase (decrease) will by definition lower (raise) welfare. Of course this would not be true in the case of more than one distoriton (defined in terms of consequences) because when the level of one distortion changes then the level of other distortions will in general not be constant.

2.3 Terms of Trade, Factor Rewards and Welfare

The relationship between terms of trade, welfare and factor rewards can now be examined. In the model under analysis there are three final goods and, therefore, three commodity prices p_1, p_2, p_3 (without any loss of generality one of these could be used as a numeraire). Obviously one can consider variations in these prices. In the first instance it is planned to vary p_3, and later p_2. Since all of the factors are not used in every sector these variations will produce results different from those established in the Heckscher-Ohlin literature.

Consider first the consequences of an increase in the price of the importable good p_3. By using the procedure outlined in section 2.2 the following expression can be obtained (differentiating with respect to p_3 instead of α):

$$\frac{1}{\bar{U}_1}\frac{dU}{dp_3} = \frac{dX_1}{dp_3} + \frac{p_2}{p_1}\frac{dX_2}{dp_3} + \frac{p_3}{p_1}\frac{dX_3}{dp_3} - \frac{M_3}{p_1} - \frac{\bar{K}^F}{p_1}\frac{dr_F}{dp_3} \qquad (2.25)$$

This simplifies to the following expression after substituting values of dX_i/dp_3 (i = 1...3):

28

$$\frac{1}{U_1}\frac{dU}{dp_3} = \frac{(\alpha-1)w_2 L_2}{k_2^F}\frac{dk_2^F}{dp_3} - \frac{M_3}{P_1} - \frac{\bar{K}^F}{P_1}\frac{dr_F}{dp_3} \qquad (2.26)$$

where

$$\frac{dk_2^F}{dp_3} = -\frac{k_1^d(f_3 - k_3^d f_3')}{\alpha p_2 k_2^F f_2''(k_1^d - k_3^d)}$$

and

$$\frac{dr_f}{dp_3} = -\frac{k_1^d(f_3 - k_3^d f_3')}{\alpha k_2^F(k_1^d - k_3^d)} \, .$$

Several propositions can be derived from equation (2.26). However, major attention can be directed to those cases which appear to be relatively more appealing in the context of colonial and third world countries. First, it is assumed that the importable sector is more capital intensive than the exportable sector. It follows that:

$$k_1^d - k_3^d < 0 \quad (k_3^d > k_1^d).$$

Second, it is assumed that $\alpha < 1$ (in other words the foreign firms pay a higher wage than the local ones). Given these assumptions it follows that:

$$\frac{dk_2^F}{dp_3} > 0$$

$$\frac{dr_F}{dp_3} > 0$$

$$(\alpha-1) < 0.$$

It therefore follows that in expression (2.26) all the terms are negative - so welfare unambiguously declines as a consequence of a rise in the price of the importable commodity. In effect a deterioration in the terms of trade results in a loss in national welfare provided that:

29

$$k_1^d < k_3^d$$

and

$$\alpha < 1.$$

This is a well known result which generally does not hold in the presence of a wage differential (or indeed, in the presence of other distortions).[8]   In the case cited above it holds only for specific restrictions.   It can easily be shown that for $\alpha > 1$ or/and other rankings of physical capital intensities, a deterioration in the terms of trade in general does not lead to a decline in welfare.

The more interesting consequences in the system under consideration are for income distribution. The formal expressions for these changes are given below:

$$\frac{dw}{dp_3} = \frac{k_1^d(f_3 - k_3^d f_3')}{(k_1^d - k_3^d)} \qquad (2.27)$$

$$\frac{dr_F}{dp_3} = -\frac{k_1^d(f_3 - k_3^d f_3')}{\alpha k_2^F(k_1^d - k_3^d)} \qquad (2.28)$$

$$\frac{d\pi}{dp_3} = -\frac{(f_3 - k_3^d f_3')}{(k_1^d - k_3^d)} \qquad (2.29)$$

These equations imply the following proposition :

Proposition 2.4: An increase in the price of the importable commodity raises (lowers) the rental on domestic capital and foreign capital provided that:

$$k_1^d - k_3^d < 0 \ (k_1^d - k_3^d > 0).$$

Such an increase in price raises (lowers) the wage rate provided that:

$$k_1^d - k_3^d > 0 \ (k_1^d - k_3^d < 0).$$

This is an exceedingly interesting result. First, the movement in the real wages is always in the opposite direction to the movement in both domestic and foreign rental on capital.[9] Second, the movement in the domestic and foreign rental on capital is always in the same direction. Third, (since p_3 represents the price of the importable good an increase in this price is equivalent to the imposition of a tariff) the demand for protection, given the assumption that:

$$k_1^d < k_3^d$$

comes from the owners of domestic and foreign capital. The interests of local and foreign capitalists are on the same side and hence for similar policy. This result shows that not only the foreign capitalists are interested in domestic policy interventions, but can also obtain local support and hence confirms the view that foreign policy intervention is generally not lacking in local support.

It is now appropriate to analyse the implications of an increae in the price of the exportable good using foreign capital for welfare and factor rewards. By following the procedures used earlier the following expressions are obtained:

$$\frac{1}{U_1} \frac{dU}{dp_2} = \frac{(\alpha - 1)L_2}{k_2^F} \frac{dk_2^F}{dp_2} - \frac{D_2}{p_1} \qquad (2.30)$$

where

$$\frac{dk_2^F}{dp_2} = \frac{f_2 - k_2^F f_2'}{p_2 k_2^F f_2''} < 0.$$

$$\frac{dr_F}{dp_2} = \frac{f_2}{k_2^F} \qquad (2.31)$$

$$\frac{d\pi}{dp_2} = 0 \qquad (2.32)$$

$$\frac{dw}{dp_2} = 0 \qquad\qquad (2.33)$$

It is best to analyse the above results by dividing them according to distortions. First, take the case when $\alpha = 1$, then it follows:

$$\frac{1}{U_1} \frac{dU}{dp_2} = - \frac{D_2}{P_1} \qquad\qquad (2.34)$$

Equation (2.34) shows that welfare falls as a result of an increase in the price of the exportable good, given the presence of monopoly power in trade of capital. This result is the same as the one obtained in Chapter 1 and requires no further explanation. The only ancillary remark that might be made is that the result of Chapter 1 holds in a more general framework which includes importables and allows for diminishing returns to labour.

Now, suppose that both distortions are present. Furthermore, we assume that $\alpha < 1$ implying that foreign firms pay more than local firms. Then it is clear that the first term in equation (2.30) is positive and the second negative; and the total effect is ambiguous. The intuitive explanation of the ambiguity follows. Let us analyse the term:

$$((\alpha - 1)L_2/k_2^F)\ dk_2^F/dp_2 .$$

This represents a productivity gain to the economy on account of movement of labour into sector 2. This is so because $\alpha < 1$, therefore $w_2 > w$. Price of commodity 2 has increased therefore output of X_2 increases and labour moves from low productivity to a high productivity sector. Such a movement of labour represents a gain for the economy. The second term reflects the effect of change in the price of commodity 2 on repatriation payments. This is always negative because the rental on foreign capital always rises when the price of commodity 2 increases. This is clear from equation (2.31). The total effect depends on the relative magnitude of these two opposing forces. Finally, note that an increase in the price of commodity 2 results in gains for foreign factors and absolutely no gains for the local factors. This brings to an end the discussion of the relationship between terms of trade, welfare and factor rewards. Additional comments on these issues will be made towards the end of this chapter.

32

2.4 Economic Expansion and Welfare

It is now appropriate to analyse the consequences of economic expansion on welfare in the presence of two distortions: (i) wage differential and (ii) monopoly power in trade of foreign-owned capital. Economic expansion in the system under consideration can occur either due to factor accumulation and/or technical progress. These types of expansion are not mutually exclusive but for analytical and pedagogic convenience they will be treated separately. The analysis will initially focus on the effects of factor accumulation.

The model established has three factors of production, labour, domestic capital and foreign capital. These factors of production can be distinguished from two different viewpoints. First, they can be judged from the perspective of mobility. One factor (labour) is fully mobile, one partially mobile (domestic capital) and one factor specific (foreign capital). Second, the factors can be distinguished from the point of view of national and foreign ownership. Two factors (labour and domestic capital) are owned domestically and the third factor (foreign capital) is foreign owned. It is not intended to analyse the impact of all these types of factor accumulation on welfare. Only the impact of foreign capital accumulation and growth in the labour force on welfare will be considered. While the growth of the labour force will capture the impact of a domestic fully mobile factor on welfare; the growth of foreign-owned capital will capture the impact of foreign ownership and factor specificity on welfare.

Consider initially the effect of an increase in the labour force on welfare, at constant commodity prices. By differentiating the utility function with respect to labour and by following the procedure outlined earlier, the expression given below is obtained:

$$\frac{1}{U_1} \frac{dU}{d\bar{L}} = \frac{dX_1}{d\bar{L}} + \frac{P_2}{P_1} \frac{dX_2}{d\bar{L}} + \frac{P_3}{P_1} \frac{dX_3}{d\bar{L}} \qquad (2.35)$$

The solutions for $dX_i/d\bar{L}$ $(i = 1...3)$ can easily be obtained by differentiating the appropriate equations. By substituting these solutions and on simplifying, this can be reduced to:

33

$$\frac{1}{U_1} \frac{dU}{d\bar{L}} = w \qquad\qquad (2.36)$$

Since w represents the wage rate, $(1/U_1)(dU/d\bar{L})$ is always positive.

Proposition 2.5: In this model where the wage rate is identical as between two sectors not using the specific factor (foreign-owned capital), an increase in the supply of non-specific factors always increases welfare. These factors are also domestically owned. [11]
The above proposition has a bearing on the following statement of Bhagwati and on a theorem of Hazari (7). According to Bhagwati (3), [page 81, Proposition 4], "For each kind of distortion, growth may be immiserizing". This can be referred to as a statement rather than as proposition 4 because it is not logically falsifiable and, in that sense, is not a proposition. In Hazari (7), [page 197, Theorem 4] it is stated, "Economic expansion does not necessarily raise welfare in the presence of (i), (ii), (iii) and (v)". The numbers (i), (ii), (iii) and (v) refer to: factor price differentials, minimum real wage rates, Meade-type production externalities and tariff distortion in the small country case. This theorem is based on the two-by-two model. Proposition 2.5 shows that Hazari's result does not necessarily hold in a more than two goods model.
An intuitive explanation of Proposition 2.5 might run along the following lines. At constant commodity prices, an increase in the supply of non-specific factors has no bearing on the output of the sector using the specific factor. This is easily seen by examining the factor employment conditions. An increase in the non-specific factor leaves $\bar{K}^F$ unchanged. Hence, by equation (2.16), $k_2^F L_2$ must remain unchanged. At constant prices k_2^F cannot change, hence, L_2 also must remain fixed. Since neither k_2^F nor L_2 can change, as a consequence of an increase in the non-specific factors, output of X_2 will be constant. So the result of a change in non-specific factors on welfare depends on the output responses of sectors 1 and 3. These sectors are non-distorted, hence, the result shown by equation (2.36) is validated.
Proposition 2.5 is of considerable interest. This proposition shows that certain types of growth will never lead to immiserization in spite of the

presence of distortions. The absence of the count-
erpart of Proposition 2.5 in the standard two-by-two
model may be further explained by examining the
following general expression relating change in
welfare to an expansionary agent Θ, at constant
prices:

$$\frac{dU}{U_1} = \frac{\partial X_1}{\partial \Theta} d\Theta + \frac{P_2}{P_1} \frac{\partial X_2}{\partial \Theta} d\Theta + \frac{P_3}{P_1} \frac{\partial X_3}{\partial \Theta} d\Theta$$

In a three sector model the presence of a wage
differential need not create a wedge between marginal
rates of factor substitution in every pair of
sectors. Hence, any expansion that allows for the
absence of a wage differential to have an impact on
the marginal rates of   substitution will be non-
immiserizing. For instance, in this model, both
labour and domestic capital accumulation at constant
prices leave the output of sector 2 undisturbed.
Hence, the expression given above reduces to:

$$\frac{dU}{U_1} = \frac{\partial X_1}{\partial \Theta} d\Theta + \frac{P_3}{P_1} \frac{\partial X_3}{\partial \Theta} d\Theta$$

Since there is no distortion present between sectors
1 and 3 the normal result must follow. This cannot
happen in the standard two-by-two model because any
expansionary agent must affect the output of both
sectors.
    The impact of an increase in supply of the
specific factor foreign capital can now be examined.
By following the procedure used earlier to obtain
the impact of growth in labour supply , the
following equation can be derived to show the impact
of foreign capital accumulation on welfare:

$$\frac{1}{U_1} \frac{dU}{d\bar{K}^F} = \frac{(1 - \alpha)w_2}{k_2^F} \qquad (2.37)$$

Equation (2.37) presents us with several interesting
results; they will be considered individually.
    Suppose we assume $\alpha = 1$, i.e. the absence of a
wage differential. If $\alpha = 1$, then $(1/U_1) \, dU/d\bar{K}^F = 0$,
in other words an increase in the supply of a
foreign-owned factor has no impact on the welfare
level of the community. This happens because in the
absence of a wage differential the increase in

35

foreign capital increases welfare by the same magnitude as the rental on capital - but this is precisely equal to the rate of repatriation payments. Again this confirms the result presented in Chapter 1 in a more general framework.

Now consider the more realistic framework where firms using foreign capital pay a higher wage than the firms that use domestic capital and labour. This implies that $\alpha = 1$, hence $(1/U_1)\ dU/d\bar{K}^F > 0$. In other words, any increase in the specific factor (foreign capital) always raises welfare. This happens because an increase in foreign capital results in an expansion in sector 2 which is a high productivity sector $(w_2 > w)$. It attracts labour from the low productivity sectors, thus raising welfare. This result again poses a dilemma for the policy maker. On equity grounds this wage differential is undesirable, but from the welfare point of view it helps the country in retaining some benefit from the accumulation of the foreign owned factor of production.

It should also be added that when $\alpha > 1$ (foreign-owned firms paying less than the local wage rate), then welfare always decreases as a consequence of foreign capital accumulation. There is no dilemma regarding policy formulation in this particular case. On both equity and welfare grounds the wage differential needs to be removed. The following proposition follows from equation (2.37).

Proposition 2.6: An increase in the supply of the specific factor foreign capital at constant commodity prices increases (decreases) welfare if $\alpha < 1$ ($\alpha > 1$) and leaves welfare unchanged if $\alpha = 1$.

In Chapter 1 it was shown that foreign capital accumulation results in de-industrialization. We now show that de-industrialization may also occur in the more general framework. Suppose that commodities X_1 and X_3 are produced in the traditional sector. Therefore, the income of the traditional sector becomes:

$$I^T = X_1 + P_3 X_3 \qquad (2.38)$$

Commodity X_2 with the help of foreign-owned capital is produced in the modern or advanced sector. The income of the advanced sector becomes:

$$I^A = P_2 X_2 \qquad (2.39)$$

36

It follows by differentiating equations (2.38) and (2.39) with respect to foreign-owned capital, at constant prices:

$$\frac{dI^T}{d\bar{K}^F} = \frac{dX_1}{d\bar{K}^F} + P_3 \frac{dX_3}{d\bar{K}^F} = -\frac{w}{k_2^{\bar{F}}} \qquad (2.40)$$

$$\frac{dI^A}{d\bar{K}^F} = P_2 \frac{dX_2}{d\bar{K}^F} = \frac{P_2 f_2}{k_2^F} \qquad (2.41)$$

It is obvious from expression (2.40) that the traditional sectors decline on account of specificity of foreign-owned capital and the small country assumption. The explanation of the above result can be developed along the same lines as in Chapter 1.

The next aspect to be examined are the implications of Hicks -neutral technical progress in sector 2 - the sector using foreign capital for welfare and rewards of the factors of production. Neutral technical progress is introduced via the production function in the following manner:

$$X_2 = \lambda_2 F_2(L_2, K_2^F) = \lambda_2 L_2 f_2(k_2^F) \qquad (2.42)$$

where λ_2 is a shift factor representing Hicks - neutral technical progress. The introduction of this type of economic expansion also leads to some modification in the conditions for factor rewards. These now become:

$$w = p_1(f_1 - k_1^d f_1') = \alpha \lambda_2 p_2 (f_2 - k_2^F f_2') = p_3(f_3 - k_3^d f_3') \quad (2.43)$$

$$r_F = \lambda_2 p_2 f_2' \qquad (2.44)$$

Given equations (2.43) to (2.44) and the rest of the model, the following expressions obtain for any change in welfare resulting from technical progress in the sector using foreign capital:

$$\frac{1}{U_1} \frac{dU}{d\lambda_2} = \frac{(\alpha - 1)w_2 L_2}{k_2^F} \frac{dk_2^F}{d\lambda_2} \qquad (2.45)$$

37

where

$$\frac{dk_2^F}{d\lambda_2} = \frac{f_2 - k_2^F f_2'}{\lambda_2 k_2^F f_2''} \ < \ 0$$

Consider the case when $\alpha = 1$ implying that no distortion exists in the labour market. In this framework (2.45) reduces to:

$$\frac{1}{U_1} \frac{dU}{d\lambda_2} = 0 \qquad\qquad (2.46)$$

Proposition 2.7: Technical progress in the sector using foreign capital always leaves welfare unchanged in the presence of monopoly power in trade of capital.
This result is again similar to that obtained for accumulation of foreign-owned capital and therefore does not need to be commented upon.

Proposition 2.8: Welfare increases (decreases) as a result of technical progress depending upon $\alpha < 1$ ($\alpha > 1$).
This is a most fascinating theorem. Immiserizing growth (normal growth) simply depends on the direction of the differential. When $\alpha < 1$ (the sector using foreign capital pays a higher wage) welfare always rises and when $\alpha > 1$ (the domestic sector pays a higher wage) welfare always declines. The explanation of this result is the same as for capital accumulation and need not be repeated here.
Finally note the distributional consequences of technical progress:

$$\frac{dw}{d\lambda_2} = 0 \qquad\qquad (2.47)$$

$$\frac{d\pi}{d\lambda_2} = 0 \qquad\qquad (2.48)$$

$$\frac{dr_F}{d\lambda_2} = \frac{p_2 f_2}{k_2^F} \ > \ 0 \qquad\qquad (2.49)$$

It is clear from the above equations that the factor rewards of the domestic factors do not change as a

38

consequence of technical progress in the sector
using foreign capital as a specific factor. However,
the return to the foreign-owned capital always rises
due to technical progress. This result occurs due
to the small country assumption.

The implications of Hicks- neutral technical
progress in sector 3 are now scrutinised for its
welfare and income distribution consequences.
Technical progress in sector 3 is introduced in the
following manner:

$$X_3 = \lambda_3 L_3 f_3 (k_3^d) \qquad (2.50)$$

The factor reward conditions now become:

$$w = p_1 (f_1 - k_1^d f_1') = \alpha p_2 (f_2 - k_2^F f_2') = \lambda_3 p_3 (f_3 - k_3^d f_3') \quad (2.51)$$

$$\pi = p_1 f_1' = p_3 f_3' \qquad (2.52)$$

By using the procedures already outlined the
following expression for the change in welfare as a
consequence of technical progress in sector 3 can be
written:

$$\frac{1}{U_1} \frac{dU}{d\lambda_3} = \frac{p_3}{p_1} L_3 f_3 - \frac{\bar{K}^F}{p_1} \frac{dr_F}{d\lambda_3} \qquad (2.53)$$

where

$$\frac{dr_F}{d\lambda_3} = - \frac{k_1^d p_3 f_3}{\alpha (k_1^d - k_3^d)} \gtrless 0 \text{ as } k_1^d - k_3^d \lessgtr 0$$

Equation (2.53) provides the expression that
indicates the impact of technical progress on welfare
in sector 3. This expression consists of two terms.
The first term $(p_3 L_3 f_3/p_1)$ represents the gain in
productivity due to technical progress. This gain in
productivity always raises welfare. The second term
$(-\bar{K}^F/p_1)(dr_F/d\lambda_3)$ indicates the impact of technical
progress on repatriation payments and their impact on
welfare. The sign of the second term depends on the
capital intensities of sectors 1 and 3, $dr_F/d\lambda_3 > 0$
when :

$$k_1^d - k_3^d < 0 \; (\frac{dr_F}{d\lambda_3} > 0 \text{ when } k_1^d - k_3^d < 0).$$

Suppose that:

$$\frac{dr_F}{d\lambda_3} > 0$$

implies that the return on foreign capital increases. This increase in the rental on foreign capital in turn increases the total magnitude of repatriation payments and hence, represents a loss to the economy. Since the first term is positive and the second negative, the impact of technical progress on welfare is ambiguous. 'Immiserizing growth' will occur if the following inequality is satisfied:

$$\frac{p_3}{p_1} L_3 f_3 - \frac{\bar{K}^F}{p_1} \frac{dr_F}{d\lambda_3} < 0$$

<u>Proposition 2.9</u>: Technical progress in sector 3 does not necessarily raise welfare.

It is important to emphasise the difference between Propositions 2.9 and 2.5. Domestic factor accumulation always raises welfare in spite of the presence of two distortions wage differential and monopoly power in trade of capital. However, due to the presence of uncorrected monopoly power in trade of capital welfare does not necessarily rise when technical progress occurs in the domestically-owned sector. This is indeed a disturbing result because the presence of monopoly power affects the ability of the economy to take advantage of technological progress in domestically-owned sectors to raise welfare.

2.5 Conclusions

It seems worthwhile to recapitulate on some of the results obtained and to comment on several others. First, it has been established that some of the results obtained on the basis of a simple two-sector model also obtain in the more general framework of this chapter. The proposition that a colonial economy is unable to gain from an increase in the price of the exportable commodity that uses foreign capital as a specific factor is re-confirmed. This is a rather serious finding and is obviously related to the controversy on terms of trade and welfare. It suggests that it may be erroneous to relate

40

welfare changes to terms of trade without examining the returns to foreign factor in the presence of uncorrected monopoly power in trade of capital and sector specificity of foreign capital. It has also been re-established in this chapter that economic expansion (via foreign factor accumulation and technological progress) in sector using foreign capital does not raise welfare (except for its initial impact). Thus, the story of stagnation continues to hold in a more general model. De-industrialization has also been shown to occur with foreign capital accumulation provided sectors 1 and 2 are treated as the traditional sectors.

The inflow of foreign capital has also been identified as one source of creating a wage distortion. It is well established in the literature that such distortions lead to several pathological (non-intuitive) results. Some of the more important perverse results that have been obtained due to the presence of the distortion bear repetition. First, the removal of a distortion (specifically in the case in which $w_F > w$) is not desirable from two alternative, but not mutually exclusive points of view. The removal of the distortion can be viewed as a reduction in income inequality. In this case it has been shown that in the realistic case ($\alpha < 1$) its removal raises the reward of the foreigners and therefore, they stand to gain from its removal. Moreover, its removal need not raise welfare and is therefore undesirable from an efficiency point of view. Here is the dilemma for the policy maker efficiency versus equity. It has also been shown that foreign factor accumulation raises welfare in the case in which $w_F > w$ - another reason from the efficiency point of view of not changing the distribution of income. All these are issues which concern development in the present day economies, but also may well have been present in colonial times.

The implications of changes in the price of importables on factor rewards and welfare were also considered. The result on factor rewards lends support to the view that capitalists have similar interests whether they be of domestic origin or foreign; and their interests conflict with those of labour. Moreover, it was also shown that on account of the above link, the foreign capitalists have an interest in the policies of the host country. This result in some ways is analogous to that obtained in the previous chapter where the foreigners (colonisers) were interested in following a policy of

laissez-fare, contrary to the interests of the
colony.

Finally, notice the absence of taxation of
returns on capital (domestic and foreign) in the
model. If the earnings are taxed (for example in
Fiji the rate of corporation tax is 33% both for
domestic and foreign capital), then this provides
yet another source of policy induced distortion and
hence, under certain conditions, would reinforce
results already obtained. Therefore, the neglect of
corporation tax is in fact not a serious matter.

NOTES

1. This chapter is a revised and expanded
version of my paper with Professor P.K. Pattanaik on
"Some Welfare Propositions in a Three Commodity,
Three Factor Model of Trade in the Presence of
Foreign-Owned Factors of Production", *Greek Economic
Review*, Vol.2 (1980) 12-23.

2. The wage differential is regarded as
distortionary when it cannot be explained on
legitimate economic grounds. For a discussion of
possible sources of such distortions see: Bhagwati
and Ramaswami (2) and Magee (13). The inflow of
foreign capital creating a wage distortion was first
discussed in a paper by Hazari and Pattanaik (8).

3. This contrasts with the approach adopted by
Bhagwati (3) in his classic paper on distortion
theory, in which distortions are defined in terms of
consequences. He defines four principal types of
distortions, namely, (i) FRT $\neq$ DRT = DRS: (ii) DRT $\neq$
DRS = FRT; (iii) DRS $\neq$ DRT = FRT and (iv) non-
operation on the efficient production possibility
curve. Thus, the number of distortions is determined not in terms of intuitive sources but in terms of
consequences. A critique of this approach is
developed in Hazari (7).

4. This model is similar to that set up by
Corden and Gruen (4).

5. It is often asserted in development
literature that the colonial regimes are interested
in mainting income inequalities. This is so on
account of colonies being an extension of capitalist
development. This model shows that such a desire
need not necessarily emerge on account of economic
factors.

6. For example, several expatriates in Fiji pay
a higher wage to the house-girls than local people.

7. The following footnote in Bhagwati's paper
makes this point very clearly: "Unlike the case of a

constant wage differential, which also leads to distortion 2 (DRT ≠ DRS = FRT) in addition to Distortion 4 (*non-operation on the efficient production possibility curve*), we can devise a variable tax-cum-subsidy that satisfies the constraint on factor employment while creating only Distortion 4". (Footnote 13, page 78, emphasis added).

8. See Batra and Pattanaik (1) and Hazari (5), (7).

9. This need not be the case in the presence of factor specificity. It has been shown by Hazari that the rental on a specific factor and wage rates may move in the same direction and therefore the class conflict may take the form of specific factor owners and workers versus the owners of non-specific capital, see Chapter 4 of this book.

10. This result does not follow in the presence of a wage differential. On account of value intensity reversals output may respond perversely to a change in its price - see Hazari (7). In the model we are considering (and for $w = \alpha \; w_F$) this cannot occur because value intensity reversals are not logically possible. These reversals could arise if the wage rates between sector 1 and sector 3 were not equal.

11. A result similar to this proposition has also been obtained in the non-traded goods framework - see Hazari and Sgro (7) and Hazari, Sgro and Suh (10).

12. In the standard trade model technical progress may result in immiserizing growth due to perverse response of output to technical progress and/or the inequality between the domestic rate of transformation and the foreign rate of transformation (this inequality reflects the direction of the differential), see Hazari (6), (7).

REFERENCES

(1)   Batra, R.N. and Pattanaik, P.K. 1971. Factor Market Imperfections: The Terms of Trade and Welfare. *American Economic Review*, Vol. 61 (December) 946-55.
(2)   Bhagwati, J.N. and Ramaswami, V.K. 1963. Domestic Distortions, Tariffs and the Theory of Optimum Subsidy. *Journal of Political Economy*, Vol.71 (February) 44-50.
(3)   Bhagwati, J.N. 1971. The Generalised Theory of Distortions and Welfare. In J.N. Bhagwati, R. Jones, R. Mundell and J. Vanek (eds.), *Trade, Balance of Payments and Growth. Papers in International Economics in Honour of Charles P.*

Kindleberger. Amsterdam, North Holland.

(4) Corden, W.M. and Gruen, F.H. 1970. A Tariff that Worsens the Terms of Trade. In I. MacDougall and R. Snape (eds.), *Studies in International Economics*. Amsterdam, North Holland.

(5) Hazari, B.R. 1974. Factor Market Distortions and Gains from Trade Revisited. *Weltwirtschafliches Archiv*, Vol.110 (October) 413-29.

(6) ────── 1975. Factor Market Distortions, Technical Progress and Trade. *Oxford Economic Papers*, Vol.27, (March) 47-60.

(7) ────── 1978. *The Pure Theory of International Trade and Distortions*. London: Croom Helm.

(8) Hazari, B.R. and Pattanaik, P.K. 1980. Some Welfare Propositions in a Three Commodity, Three Factor Model of Trade in the Presence of Foreign-Owned Factors of Production. *Greek Economic Review*, Vol.2 (April) 12-23.

(9) Hazari, B.R. and Sgro, P.M. 1980. Theorems on Immiserizing Growth (Normal Growth) in the Non-Traded Goods and Wage Differential Framework: An Extension. *Southern Economic Journal*, Vol.47 (July) 241-43.

(10) Hazari, B.R., Sgro, P.M. and Suh, D.C. 1981. *Non-Traded and Intermediate Goods and the Pure Theory of International Trade*. London: Croom Helm.

(11) Hicks, J.R. 1932. *The Theory of Wages*. London: Macmillan and Company.

(12) Magee, S.P. 1971. Factor Market Distortions, Production, Distribution and the Pure Theory of International Trade. *Quarterly Journal of Economics*, Vol.85 (November) 623-43.

(13) ────── 1973. Factor Market Distortions and Trade: A Survey. *Oxford Economic Papers*, Vol.25 (March) 1-43.

(14) ────── 1976. *International Trade and Distortions in Factor Markets*. Business Economic and Finance Series, Vol.6. New York and Base: Marcel Dekker.

Chapter 3

FOREIGN CAPITAL, NON-TRADED GOODS, CLASS CONFLICT
AND THE PURE THEORY OF TRADE

So far the models analysed have been ones in which
all goods are traded internationally and foreign
capital is sector specific. It is now proposed to
introduce a non-traded goods sector[1] and also
partial mobility of foreign-owned capital. Foreign-
owned capital will now be utilised by the export
sector and the non-traded goods sector along with
domestic labour. The remaining two sectors will
produce using only domestic labour and domestic
capital.

As far as the author is aware, no paper in
trade theory has incorporated the presence of a
partially mobile foreign-owned factor of production
in the non-traded goods sector.[2] This has been so
in spite of the increasing volume of literature that
has appeared on the role of such factors in the
real theory of trade.[3] The object of this chapter
is partly to fulfil this lacuna in the literature.
However, this is not the main motivation which, in
fact is occasioned by the desire to make the previous
models more realistic, as well as to test the
robustness of results already obtained. A major
point of interest will be to examine output-endowment commodity price-factor price relationships,
including changes in welfare. The relationship
between commodity prices and factor prices should
provide insights into the demand for protection by
various groups in the economy. It might be added
that foreign factors of production are often used in
the non-traded goods sector - for example by the
University of the South Pacific in Fiji.

3.1 The Model

In order to facilitate derivations, it is intended
to use the framework of activity analysis.[4] Only

45

those equations will be presented that require change and/or rewriting in the above framework. The social utility function is now given by:

$$U = U(D_1, D_2, D_3, D_N) \qquad (3.1)$$

where D_N denotes the consumption of the non-traded commodity. The other variables have been defined already in the previous chapters. The function is assumed to possess the properties already listed in Chapter 1.

Given the assumption of utility maximization it follows that:

$$\frac{U_1}{P_1} = \frac{U_2}{P_2} = \frac{U_3}{P_3} = \frac{U_N}{P_N} \qquad (3.2)$$

This equation indicates the first order equilibrium condition for obtaining maximum welfare.

In addition to the market clearing equations already presented in Chapter 2, it is now required that:

$$D_N = X_N \qquad (3.3)$$

This equation states that for the non-traded goods sector to be in equilibrium the demand for this good must equal its supply - in other words this market must clear locally.

The non-traded good, X_N, is produced with the help of domestic labour and foreign owned capital. The production function for this sector is given below:

$$X_N = F_N(L_N, K_N^F) \qquad (3.4)$$

This function is assumed to be linearly homogeneous. It is further assumed that there are diminishing returns to both factors.

Let a_{ij}s denote variable input coefficients, then the factor endowment conditions can be written as:

$$a_{L1}X_1 + a_{L2}X_2 + a_{L3}X_3 + a_{LN}X_N = \bar{L} \qquad (3.5)$$

$$a_{K1}^d X_1 \qquad\qquad + a_{K3}^d X_3 \qquad\qquad = \bar{K}^d \qquad (3.6)$$

$$a_{K2}^F X_2 + a_{KN}^F X_N = \bar{K}_N^F \qquad (3.7)$$

Note that sectors 1 and 3 use domestic labour and domestic capital while sectors 2 and N use domestic labour and foreign capital. Foreign capital is now partially mobile and can be used in sector 2 and sector N. Thus, the assumption of sector specificity of foreign capital has been relaxed.

Given the assumptions of perfect competition, incomplete specialisation and profit maximization it follows that the unit cost of production must equal price. Furthermore, it is assumed that $w_1 = w_3 = w$ and $w_2 = w_N = w_F$; and $w = \alpha\, w_F$ for $\alpha \neq 1$ ($\alpha > 0$). The pricing equations then become:

$$a_{L1}w + a_{K1}^d \pi = p_1 \qquad (3.8)$$

$$a_{L2}w_F + a_{K2}^F r_{F'} = p_2 \qquad (3.9)$$

$$a_{L3}w + a_{K3}^d \pi = p_3 \qquad (3.10)$$

$$a_{LN}w_F + a_{KN}^F r_F = p_N \qquad (3.11)$$

It is again assumed that the country is small so that p_1, p_2 and p_3 are supplied exogenously.

Finally equations are needed to determine a_{ij}s the variable input coefficients - these are given below:

$$a_{Lj} = a_{Lj}\ (w, \pi) \qquad j = 1,3 \qquad (3.12)$$

$$a_{Kj}^d = a_{Kj}^d\ (w, \pi) \qquad j = 1,3 \qquad (3.13)$$

$$a_{Lj} = a_{Lj}\ (w_F, r_F) \qquad j = 2, N \qquad (3.14)$$

$$a_{Kj}^F = a_{Kj}^F\ (w_F, r_F) \qquad j = 2, N \qquad (3.15)$$

This completes the specification of the model.

3.2 Changes in Commodity Prices, Factor Rewards and Welfare

This section is devoted to an analysis of the consequences of changes in commodity prices on factor rewards and national welfare. The basic outline is a four commodity model in which three commodity prices are given exogenously - the price of the two exportable commodities and one importable commodity. The price of the non-traded good is determined endogenously. At the outset it is important to provide general expressions for all price changes and then analyse specific cases. By differentiating equations (3.8) to (3.11) totally, the following outcomes emerge:

$$\Theta_{L1} \hat{w} + \Theta_{K1}^{d} \hat{\pi} = \hat{p}_1 - w \hat{a}_{L1} - \pi \hat{a}_{K1}^{d} \qquad (3.16)$$

$$\Theta_{L2} \hat{w}_F + \Theta_{K2}^{F} \hat{r}_F = \hat{p}_2 - w_F \hat{a}_{L2} - r_F \hat{a}_{K2}^{F} \qquad (3.17)$$

$$\Theta_{L3} \hat{w} + \Theta_{K1}^{d} \hat{\pi} = \hat{p}_3 - w \hat{a}_{L3} - r_F \hat{a}_{K3}^{d} \qquad (3.18)$$

$$\Theta_{LN} \hat{w}_F + \Theta_{KN}^{F} \hat{r}_F = \hat{p}_N - w_F \hat{a}_{LN} - r_F \hat{a}_{KN}^{F} \qquad (3.19)$$

where Θ_{ij}s denote relative shares (for example, $\Theta_{L1} = a_{L1} w/p_1$) and ^s denote relative change (for example $\hat{p}_1 = dp_1/p_1$). From cost minimising conditions it is known that the sum of changes in the coefficients equal zero. By utilising this property and solving the system contained in equations (3.16) to (3.19) we obtain:

$$\hat{w} = \frac{\hat{p}_1 \Theta_{K3}^{d} - \Theta_{K1}^{d} \hat{p}_3}{|\Theta|} \qquad (3.20)$$

$$\hat{\pi} = \frac{\Theta_{L1} \hat{p}_3 - \Theta_{L3} \hat{p}_1}{|\Theta|} \qquad (3.21)$$

where

$$|\Theta| = \begin{vmatrix} \Theta_{L1} & \Theta_{K1}^d \\ \Theta_{L3} & \Theta_{K3}^d \end{vmatrix} = \frac{w\,\pi\,L_1\,L_3}{P_1\,X_1\,P_3\,X_3}\,(k_3^d - k_1^d)$$

which is positive (negative) according to:

$$k_3^d > k_1^d \quad (k_3^d < k_1^d).$$

It is known that $w = \alpha\,w_F$, therefore $\hat{w} = \hat{w}_F$ and further, a solution for $\hat{w}_F$ is also available from equation (3.20). Since the solution for $\hat{w}_F$ is known it follows from the above equations:

$$\hat{r}_F = \frac{\hat{P}_2}{\Theta_{K2}^F} - \frac{\Theta_{L2}}{\Theta_{K2}^F\,|\Theta|}\left[\hat{P}_1\,\Theta_{K3}^d - \Theta_{K1}^d\,\hat{P}_3\right] \qquad (3.22)$$

$$\hat{P}_N = \frac{\hat{P}_1\,\Theta_{K3}^d - \Theta_{K1}^d\,\hat{P}_3}{|\Theta|}\,\frac{(\Theta_{LN}\,\Theta_{K2}^F - \Theta_{KN}^F\,\Theta_{L2})}{\Theta_{K2}^F} + \Theta_{KN}^F\,\frac{\hat{P}_2}{\Theta_{K2}^F} \qquad (3.23)$$

Equations (3.20) to (3.22) provide the general solutions for the consequences of changes in the prices of commodities 1,2 and 3 on the wage rate, return on domestic capital, the return on foreign capital and the price of the non-traded good. Having obtained the general solution it is easy to deal with specific cases.

First consider the impact of a change in the price of the exportable commodity (the sector using foreign-owned capital) on factor prices and the price of the non-traded good. This is accomplished by setting $\hat{p}_1 = 0$, $\hat{p}_3 = 0$. It follows that:

$$\hat{w} = 0 \qquad (3.24)$$

$$\hat{\pi} = 0 \qquad (3.25)$$

$$\hat{r}_F = \frac{\hat{P}_2}{\Theta_{K2}^F} \qquad (3.26)$$

49

$$\hat{P}_N = \frac{\Theta^F_{KN}}{\Theta^F_{K2}}\; \hat{P}_2 \qquad\qquad (3.27)$$

From equations (3.26) and (3.27) it is clear that an increase in the price of the exportable commodity using foreign capital always raises the rate of return on foreign capital and will therefore lower welfare in view of the fact that $\hat{w} = 0$ and $\hat{\pi} = 0$.[5] This re-confirms the results already reported in Chapters 1 and 2 in a less general framework. The change in the price of the exportable good also affects the price of the non-traded good which always rises as a result of an increase in the price of the exportable good.[6] This result of course hinges on the assumption that foreign capital is mobile between the non-traded and the exportable goods sector.

Now consider the consequences of a change in the price of the importable good. This is done by setting $\hat{p}_1$ and $\hat{p}_2$ equal to zero. The factor price changes are now given by the following expressions:

$$\hat{w} = -\frac{\Theta^d_{K1}\;\hat{P}_3}{|\Theta|} \qquad\qquad (3.28)$$

$$\hat{\pi} = \frac{\Theta_{L1}\;\hat{P}_3}{|\Theta|} \qquad\qquad (3.29)$$

$$\hat{r}_F = \frac{\Theta_{L2}\;\Theta^d_{K1}}{\Theta^F_{K2}\;|\Theta|}\;\hat{P}_3 \qquad\qquad (3.30)$$

The price of non-traded good also changes which becomes:

$$\hat{P}_N = -\frac{\Theta^d_{K1}\;\hat{P}_3}{|\Theta|}\left(\Theta_{LN}\;\Theta^F_{K2} - \Theta^F_{KN}\;\Theta_{L2}\right) \qquad\qquad (3.31)$$

From the earlier discussion it is known that $|\Theta| > 0$ $(|\Theta| < 0)$ according to :

$$k_3^d > k_1^d \quad (k_3^d < k_1^d)$$

it follows that the rental on foreign and domestic capital always move in the same direction.[7] The wage rate moves in the opposite direction to the rentals on capital. Thus as shown in Chapter 2 the class conflict is between workers and capitalists both domestic and foreign. As can be seen from equation (3.31) the price of non-traded good may rise or fall depending on the factor intensity rankings of sectors 1 and 2 and sectors 2 and N.

The task that remains to be accomplished is to obtain the welfare consequences of a change in the price of the importable commodity. By using the procedure outlined earlier, the following expression for a change in welfare is obtained (as a consequence of a change in the price of commodity 3):

$$\frac{1}{\bar{U}_1} \frac{dU}{dp_3} = (1 - \beta) \frac{p_2}{p_1} \frac{dX_2}{dp_3} + (1 - \gamma) \frac{p_N}{p_1} \frac{dX_N}{dp_3} - \frac{M_3}{p_1} - \bar{K}^F \frac{dr_F}{dp_3} \qquad (3.32)$$

where

$$\beta = \frac{w \; dL_2 + r_F \; dK_2^F}{w_F \; dL_2 + r_F \; dK_2^F}$$

and

$$\gamma = \frac{w \; dL_N + r_F \; dK_N^F}{w_F \; dL_N + r_F \; dK_N^F} \; .$$

It is clear that β and γ are both less than one (greater than one) according to $w_F > w$ ($w_F < w$).

It is now possible to analyse the consequences of a change in the price of the importable good on welfare. First, consider the case in which there is no wage distortion: $\alpha = \beta = 1$. In this case equation (3.32) reduces to:

$$\frac{1}{\bar{U}_1} \frac{dU}{dp_3} = - \frac{M_3}{p_1} - \bar{K}^F \frac{dr_F}{dp_3} \qquad (3.33)$$

The first term in equation (3.33) is always negative. The return on foreign capital, dr_F/dp_3, rises (falls)

according to the capital intensity of sector 3
vis-à-vis sector 1, that is:

$$k_3^d > k_1^d \ (k_3^d < k_1^d).$$

Thus if it is assumed that the importable sector is
more capital-intensive than the exportable sector
then $(1/U_1)(dU/dp_3)$ is unambiguously negative and,
therefore, welfare declines as a result of a
deterioration in the terms of trade. It is
important to note that the decline in welfare
depends on two effects: one the standard terms of
trade effect denoted by the term $- M_3/p_1$, and other
the effect of uncorrected monopoly power in trade of
capital shown by:

$$\bar{K}^F \left(\frac{dr_F}{dp_3}\right).$$

This second effect arises because the rental on
foreign capital rises as a result of a change in the
price of the importable good. In the case of:

$$k_3^d > k_1^d$$

both effects work against the colony (host country).
It should be emphasised here that one cannot
assert the proposition that the deterioration in the
terms of trade (in the presence of uncorrected
monopoly power in trade of capital) leads to a loss
greater than that under its absence. This erroneous
conclusion may be derived by asserting that:

$$- \frac{M_3}{P_1} - \bar{K}^F \frac{dr_F}{dp_3} < - \frac{M_3}{P_1} \tag{3.34}$$

This need not be the case because the term $- M_3/p_1$
is derived from two different models (one with
uncorrected monopoly power in trade of capital and
the other without the presence of such monopoly
power) which need not result in the same equilibrium
values of the variable $(- M_3/p_1)$. However, if
equation (3.34) holds then uncorrected monopoly
power in trade of capital imposes a further burden
on the colonial (host) economy as a result of
deterioration in the terms of trade.
It is important to emphasise that it is not
necessary for welfare to fall as a result of

deterioration in the terms of trade in the presence
of uncorrected monopoly power in trade of capital.
Suppose that:

$$k^d_3 < k^d_1$$

it follows that $dr_F/dp_3 < 0$ implying the positivity
of the second term in equation (3.33). Therefore,
welfare rises if the following condition is
satisfied:

$$- \frac{M_3}{p_1} - \bar{K}^F \frac{dr_F}{dp_3} > 0$$

This result demonstrates the inability of colonies
(today's third world countries) to take advantage of
an improvement in the terms of trade due to the
presence of uncorrected monopoly power in trade of
capital.

The above result may also occur in the presence
of a wage differential along with uncorrected
monopoly power in trade. This is an extension of a
similar result in trade and distortion literature.[8]
More specific interpretations of expression (3.32)
are left for the enthusiastic reader. These results
cast serious doubts regarding the welfare effects of
trade liberalisation in the presence of market
imperfections.

3.3 Output-Endowment Theorems and Welfare

It is appropriate now to analyse the consequences of
factor accumulation for the levels of output; and
later link these output changes to welfare. By
differentiating equations (3.5) to (3.7) at constant
commodity prices, that is p_1, p_2, p_3 and p_N, the
following expressions are obtained:

$$\lambda_{L1} \hat{X}_1 + \lambda_{L2} \hat{X}_2 + \lambda_{L3} \hat{X}_3 = \hat{L} - \lambda_{LN} \hat{X}_N \qquad (3.35)$$

$$\lambda^d_{K1} \hat{X}_1 + \lambda^d_{K3} \hat{X}_3 \qquad = \hat{K}^d \qquad (3.36)$$

$$\lambda^F_{K2} \hat{X}_2 \qquad = \hat{K}^F - \lambda^F_{KN} \hat{X}_N \qquad (3.37)$$

where λ_{ij} is the proportion of the ith factor

53

employed in the jth commodity and ^s denote
proportional change. For example:

$$\lambda_{L1} = a_{L1} X_1/\bar{L} \quad \text{and} \quad \hat{X}_1 = dX_1/X_1.$$

It is clear from equation (3.37) that:

$$\hat{X}_2 = \frac{\hat{K}^F}{\lambda^F_{K2}} - \frac{\lambda^F_{KN}}{\lambda^F_{K2}} \hat{X}_N \tag{3.38}$$

It is known that:

$$X_N = D_N \; (p_1, \; p_2, \; p_3, \; p_N, \; I) \tag{3.39}$$

where I denotes income. From the factor side income
equality is expressed:

$$I = w(L_1 + L_3) + w_F(L_2 + L_N) + \pi \; \bar{K}^d \tag{3.40}$$

In order to keep the analysis simple initially it is
assumed that $w = w_F$ so that:

$$I = w \; \bar{L} + \pi \; \bar{K}^d \tag{3.41}$$

At constant prices it is clear that:

$$\frac{1}{U_1} \frac{dU}{d\bar{K}^F} = \frac{dI}{d\bar{K}^F} = 0 \tag{3.42}$$

$$\frac{1}{U_1} \frac{dU}{d\bar{L}} = \frac{dI}{d\bar{L}} = w \tag{3.43}$$

and

$$\frac{1}{U_1} \frac{dU}{d\bar{K}^d} = \frac{dI}{d\bar{K}^d} = \pi \tag{3.44}$$

Having obtained the expression for income changes it
follows by differentiating equation (3.39):

$$\hat{X}_N = \eta_4 \; \hat{I} \tag{3.45}$$

Equations (3.35) to (3.37) and (3.45) provide a

system of four equations in four unknowns. Although the system can be solved for the impact of all types of accumulation (simultaneous accumulation) attention will now be focussed on an increase in a single factor. In fact detailed remarks will be confined to the case of foreign capital accumulation. The results for other types of accumulation will be presented without comment. By using equations (3.35) to (3.37) and (3.42) and (3.45) the following results obtain:

$$\hat{X}_N = 0 \tag{3.46}$$

$$\hat{X}_2 = \frac{\hat{K}^F}{\lambda^F_{K2}} > 0 \tag{3.47}$$

$$\hat{X}_1 = - \frac{\lambda^d_{K3} \lambda_{L2}}{\lambda^F_{K2} \mid \lambda \mid} \hat{K}^F \tag{3.48}$$

$$\hat{X}_3 = \frac{\lambda_{L2} \lambda^d_{K1}}{\lambda^F_{K2} \mid \lambda \mid} \hat{K}^F \tag{3.49}$$

where

$$\mid \lambda \mid = \frac{L_1 L_3}{\bar{K}^d \bar{L}} (k^d_3 - k^d_1).$$

It is clear that the output of the non-traded good does not change because income remains constant (in spite of accumulation of foreign capital). Since prices are also constant the demand for the non-traded good cannot change and hence its output also cannot change. The output of X_2, the other sector using foreign capital, rises in a proportion greater than foreign capital accumulation. As far as the response of sectors 1 and 3 are concerned these are in line with the predictions of the Rybczynski theorem and depend on (λ) which is positive or negative according to:

$$k^d_1 - k^d_3 \gtrless 0.$$

The above result is not the same as that obtained by Komiya (10) in his important paper on non-traded goods; nor the same as the one obtained

by Hazari (4) in his work with specific factors. In
both works income changes occur and, therefore, so
does the demand and supply of non-traded goods.
Moreover with specificity it is difficult to
maintain constant prices. This difficulty does not
arise in the present model, but it should be quite
clearly noted that this is also not a model of total
specificity.

A diagram will help in explaining the above
result. The model under discussion consists of
three primary factors: labour, domestic capital and
foreign capital and four sectors, but production in
any sector only uses two factors of production.
Therefore, it is possible to utilise two Edgeworth-
Bowley boxes to represent the endowments and
sectoral outputs. In Figure 1.3 the line O_N C
represents the total supply of labour available to
the economy. The distance O_N A shows the total
amount of foreign capital available to the system.
Now suppose that the amount of labour utilised by
sector 2 and N is given by OD, then the box O_N A
O_2 D can be constructed. In this box the output of
sectors 2 and N can be determined by the point of
tangency between the isoquants (not drawn) of
sector O_2 and O_N and the prevailing factor price
ratio w/r_F. Suppose this point is indicated by E
then the slopes of the line O_N E and O_2 E denote
respectively the foreign capital intensities of
sector N and 2. Having determined the output level
of sector N and 2, the output levels of sector 1 and
3 can be determined. The amount of labour available
to sectors 1 and 3 is CD which equals O_1 C´. From
point O_1 and C´ the domestic capital endowment of
the economy can be represented to construct another
box. This box is given by O_1 B O_3 C´. The
equilibrium for sectors 1 and 3 then occurs at point
E_T (O_1 is the origin for sector 1 isoquants and O_3
the origin for sector 3   isoquants).

Now suppose that the endowment of foreign
capital increases from O_N A to O_N A´. From the
algebra already presented it is known that the
output of sector N does not change nor does the
foreign capital intensity. This implies that the
solution must be on the line O_2 E extended. This
occurs at point O_2' in Figure 1.3. This shows that
the output of sector 2 increases and sector 2 and N
now use more labour as shown by point D´. There is
less labour now available to sectors 1 and 3 whose
box now becomes O_1' B´ O_3' C". If the sectors
producing with domestic factors are regarded as
traditional, then de-industrialization again follows

Figure 1.3

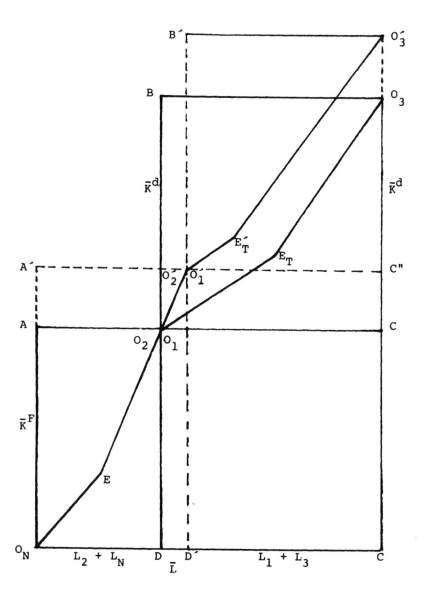

due to reallocation of labour. The output movements in these sectors are in accord with the Rybczynski theorem - the labour intensive sector contracts and the capital-intensive sector expands as is indicated by point E_T'.

In a similar manner the results for other types of accumulation can be derived. The formal expressions are given below:

Domestic Capital Accumulation:

$$\hat{X}_1 = - \frac{\hat{K}^d}{|\lambda|} \left[\frac{L_N}{\bar{L}} \frac{1}{k_2^F \lambda_{K3}^d} (k_2^F - k_N^F) \, n_4 \, s^d + \lambda_{L3} \right] \qquad (3.50)$$

$$\hat{X}_2 = - \frac{\lambda_{KN}^F}{\lambda_{K2}^F} \, n_4 \, s^d \, \hat{K}^d \quad < \quad 0 \qquad (3.51)$$

$$\hat{X}_3 = \frac{\hat{K}^d}{|\lambda|} \left[\lambda_{L1} + \frac{\lambda_{K1}^d \, L_N}{\bar{L} \, k_2^F} (k_2^F - k_N^F) \, n_4 \, s^d \right] \qquad (3.52)$$

$$\hat{X}_N = n_4 \, s^d \, \hat{K}^d \quad > \quad 0 \qquad (3.53)$$

In these equations, $s^d = \pi \, \bar{K}^d / I$, that is the share of domestic capital in national income.

Labour Accumulation:

$$\hat{X}_1 = - \frac{\lambda_{K3}^d \, L_N \, n_4 \, s^w \, (k_2^F - k_N^F)}{k_2^F \, |\lambda|} \, \hat{L} \qquad (3.54)$$

$$\hat{X}_2 = - \frac{\lambda_{KN}^F}{\lambda_{K2}^F} \, n_4 \, s^w \, \hat{L} \quad < \quad 0 \qquad (3.55)$$

$$\hat{X}_3 = \frac{\lambda_{K1}^d \, L_N \, n_4 \, s^w \, (k_2^F - k_N^F)}{k_2^F \, \bar{L} \, |\lambda|} \, \hat{L} \qquad (3.56)$$

$$\hat{X}_N = n_4 \, s^w \, \hat{L} \quad > \quad 0 \qquad (3.57)$$

In the above equations, $s^w = w\bar{L}/I$, that is the share of wages in national income.

It is clear from equations (3.50) to (3.57) that the output of the non-traded goods depends on the response of income to factor accumulation. Thus as long as there is growth (immiserising growth) it always rises (falls) as a result of domestic factor accumulation. This result, of course, requires that inferiority in consumption is ruled out. Suppose income increases. Since the stock of foreign capital is fixed when both domestic capital and labour accumulation occur, output of sector 2 must decline as it has less foreign capital at its disposal (due to expansion of the non-traded goods sector). Note that these results are not in line with the Rybczynski theorem and provide yet another example of factor-endowment theorems outside the Hecksher-Ohlin framework. Finally, the output responses of both sectors 1 and 3 not only depend on domestic capital intensities:

$$(k^d_1 - k^d_3)$$

but also on foreign capital intensities:

$$(k^F_2 - k^F_N).$$

The role of domestic capital intensities, foreign capital intensities and income in factor-endowment: output theorems is brought out in terms of Figures 2.3 and 3.3. An explanation is only developed for Figure 2.3. Suppose that the equilibrium for non-traded goods and the exportable commodities occurs at point E in the box O_N A O_2 D which shows the foreign capital endowment and the labour supply used by sectors 2 and N. The equilibrium position for sectors 1 and 3 is shown by point E_T in the box O_1 (O_2) B O_3 C' which shows the domestic capital and labour use in sectors 1 and 3. Now suppose that domestic capital expands at constant commodity and factor prices, then we know from equation (3.53) that the output of the non-traded goods sector increases. Since all prices are constant this increase must be shown by extending the foreign capital intensity ray O_N E. This is extended to E'. This results in shifting the origin O_2 (O_1) to O'_2(O'_1). The foreign capital intensity ray O'_2 E' is drawn from this origin parallel to the ray O_2 E. New equilibrium is attained at point E' which shows an increase in the

Figure 2.3

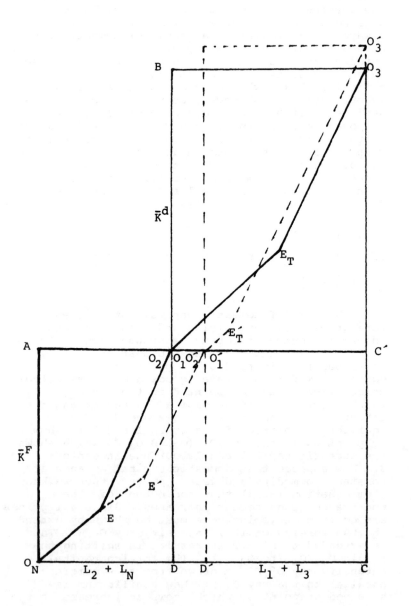

Figure 3.3

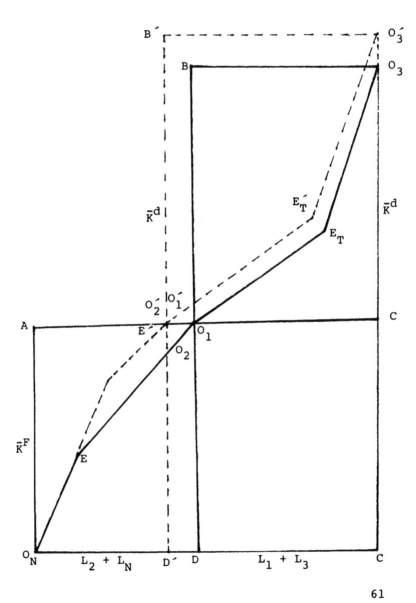

output of the non-traded good and a decline in the output of sector 2. Note that labour use by sectors N and 2 has increased from O_N D to O_N D'. The increased domestic capital endowment is shown by the distance C' O_3'. Equilibrium in sectors 3 and 1 now occurs at point E_T' where the output of sector 3 is greater and sector 1 less than at point E_T. It should be noted that these results are not the same as in the Rybczynski theorem due to the presence of income effect. This results in labour reallocation between sectors 2 and N; and sectors 3 and 1 (at constant total labour supply). Figure 3.3 shows the effect of changing the capital intensity assumptions and is self explanatory.

It is appropriate now to examine the implications of factor accumulation on welfare given the presence of both uncorrected monopoly power in trade of capital and the wage distortion $w = \alpha \, w_F$. By following the procedures outlined earlier in this work the following expressions are obtained:

$$\frac{1}{U_1} \frac{dU}{d\overline{K}^F} = \frac{(w_F - w) \, f_N}{B + (w_F - w) \, m_N \, k_N^F} \qquad (3.58)$$

$$\frac{1}{U_1} \frac{dU}{d\overline{L}} = \frac{w \, k_2^F \, f_N}{B + (w_F - w) \, m_N \, k_N^F} \qquad (3.59)$$

$$\frac{1}{U_1} \frac{dU}{d\overline{K}^d} = \frac{\pi \, k_2^F \, f_N}{B + (w_F - w) \, m_N \, k_N^F} \qquad (3.60)$$

where

$$m_N = p_N \frac{\partial D_N}{\partial I} > 0$$

and

$$B = (1 - m_N) \, w_F \, k_2^F + k_2^F \, r_F \, k_N^F + w \, k_N^F \, m_N > 0 \, .$$

Three observations are in order regarding the expressions contained in equations (3.58) to (3.60). First, all factor accumulations result in an increase in welfare if $w_F > w$. Thus from a welfare point of view the inequality in income generated through the presence of foreign ownership of capital is helpful as far as the welfare consequences of factor accumulation are concerned. Second, due to the presence of the non-traded commodity non-specific factor accumulation does not necessarily raise welfare in the presence of a wage distortion in sectors in which foreign capital is block specific. This result shows that the Hazari-Pattanaik result, regarding non-specific factor accumulation, in the presence of wage distortion does not extend to the framework of non-traded goods. Thus, the presence of non-traded goods complicates results. Third, immiserizing growth may occur when $w_F < w$ and depends on inelegant inequalities - a feature that was absent in Chapter 2.

Results relating to technical progress can also be derived. However to avoid tedious repetition these are not being presented.

3.4 Conclusions

This completes the presentation of several results pertaining to output-endowment and factor rental-commodity price relationships. The investigation has been conducted on the basis of a model that is more general than that of the previous chapters. Several results obtained previously have been re-confirmed in this more general framework. For example, an increase in the price of the exportables lowers welfare, in the presence of uncorrected monopoly power in trade of capital, on account of its impact on the return to foreign-owned factor of production. It has also been reconfirmed that class conflict takes the form of a clash between capitalists (both domestic and foreign) and workers. New results have also been obtained regarding the output-endowment and factor price-commodity price relationships. Some of these relationships do not necessarily follow from the two well known trade theorems, namely, Rybczynski and Stolper-Samuelson.

NOTES

1. A comprehensive treatment of the role of non-traded goods in the pure theory of international trade is available in Hazari-Sgro-Suh (6).
2. The role of domestically-owned specific factor in the non-traded goods sector has been analysed by Hazari (4).
3. See for example Hazari (4), Jones (8), Mussa (11).

4. This framework in trade theory has been popularised by Jones (7).
5. Note that this result is different from the Stolper-Samuelson theorem.
6. In general it is difficult to predict the direction of the movement in the relative price of the non-traded good when the terms of trade change - see for example Hazari-Sgro-Suh (6) and Komiya (10).
7. This result is more general than the well known Stolper-Samuelson theorem. This theorem in its original form applies to the case of two factors only. Some generalisations of the theorem have been obtained by Kemp (9). The interesting aspect of the generalisation in this chapter is that the owners of capital are in conflict with workers - a result that does not necessarily hold in the presence of more than two factors of production.
8. See for example Batra and Pattanaik (1) and Hazari (2), Hazari (3).

REFERENCES

(1) Batra, R.N. and Pattanaik, P.K. 1970. Domestic Distortions and the Gains from Trade. *Economic Journal*, Vol.80 (September) 638-49.
(2) Hazari, B.R. 1974. Factor Market Distortions and Gains from Trade Revisited. *Weltwietschaftliches Archiv*, Vol. 110 (October) 413-29.
(3) ———— 1978. *The Pure Theory of International Trade and Distortions*. London: Croom Helm.
(4) ———— On Specific Factors in the Non-Traded Goods Sector and Some Propositions in the Pure Theory of International Trade. Forthcoming: *Greek Economic Review*.
(5) Hazari, B.R. and Patannaik, P.K. 1980. Some Welfare Propositions in a Three Commodity Three Factor Model of Trade in the Presence of Foreign-Owned Factors of Production. *Greek Economic Review*, Vol.2 (April) 12-23.
(6) Hazari, B.R., Sgro, P.M. and Suh, D.C. 1981. *Non-Traded and Intermediate Goods and the Pure Theory of International Trade*. London: Croom Helm.
(7) Jones, R.W. 1965. The Structure of Simple General Equilibrium Models. *Journal of Political Economy*, Vol.73, (December) 7-72.
(8) ———— 1975. Income Distribution and Effective Protection in a Multi-Commodity Trade Model. *Journal of Economic Theory*, Vol.11 (August) 1-15.
(9) Kemp, M.C. 1969. *The Pure Theory of International Trade and Investment*. New Jersey: Prentice Hall.

(10) Komiya, R. 1967. Non-Traded and the Pure Theory of International Trade. *International Economic Review*, Vol.2, (June) 132-52.
(11) Mussa, M.M. 1974. Tariffs and the Distribution of Income: The Importance of Factor Specificity, Substitutability, and Intensity in the Short and Long Run. *Journal of Political Economy*, Vol.82 (November-December) 1191-1203.
(12) Rybczynski, T.M. 1955. Factor Endowments and Relative Commodity Prices. *Economica*, Vol.22 (November) 336-41.
(13) Stolper, W.F. and Samuelson, P.A. 1941. Protection and Real Wages. *Review of Economic Studies*, Vol.9 (November) 58-73.

Chapter 4

ON FOREIGN CAPITAL SPECIFICITY IN THE NON-TRADED

GOODS SECTOR AND SOME PROPOSITIONS IN THE PURE

THEORY OF INTERNATIONAL TRADE

This chapter is devoted to examining the output-
endowment and factor rental-commodity price theorems
on the basis of a model in which the foreign-owned [1]
capital is specific to the non-traded goods sector.
Thus the assumption made in the previous chapter that
foreign-owned capital is mobile between the non-
traded goods sector and the exportable sector is
dropped. Furthermore the model of the previous
chapter is also converted to a three sector model -
more specifically to the Heckscher-Ohlin framework
with a non-traded good[2] that uses sector specific
foreign capital.[3] The output-endowment and factor-
rental-commodity price relationships are also used
to examine the welfare implications of changes in
endowments and commodity prices.
    The assumption of factor specificity in the non-
traded goods sector has important implications
regarding the fixed price assumption (used in factor
endowment theorems) and often used in trade models
with non-traded goods. With the above type of
specificity, it is generally not possible to maintain
the assumption that all prices are fixed when factor
endowments change. Only the terms of trade can be
kept constant in the analysis. The price of the non-
traded good and the rental on the specific factor
both change whenever there is a change in factor
endowment. The only case in which these prices can
be held constant is when it is assumed that the
marginal product of both the non-specific and
specific factor is constant in the non-traded goods
sector. This particular assumption will be used for
some results reported in this chapter for illustrat-
ive purposes. All results obtained in this chapter
will be compared with those of the previous chapters
and of Chapter 3 in particular.

4.1 The Model

The social utility function presented in the previous chapter is now amended to exclude the consumption of one of the commodities. Hence the utility function now becomes:

$$U = U(D_2, D_3, D_N) \qquad (4.1)$$

where D_i ($i = 2,3,N$) represents the domestic consumption of three commidities, X_2, X_3 and X_N. Sector 1 has been dropped from the analysis. The utility function is again assumed to be strictly concave.

Given utility maximization it follows that in equilibrium:

$$\frac{U_2}{P_2} = \frac{U_3}{P_3} = \frac{U_N}{P_N} \qquad (4.2)$$

It is further assumed that the second commodity is partly exported, the third commodity partly imported and commodity N not traded internationally. Therefore, the market clearing conditions require that:

$$D_2 = X_2 - E_2 \qquad (4.3)$$

$$D_3 = X_3 + M_3 \qquad (4.4)$$

$$D_N = X_N \qquad (4.5)$$

The value of X_i ($i = 2,3,N$) represents the production of these commodities, the value of E_2 exports and M_3 imports.

In contrast to the previous chapters it will be here assumed that both the importable and the exportable commodities are produced with the help of labour and domestic capital. The non-traded good, it will be assumed, is produced with the aid of domestic labour and foreign-owned capital. All the production functions are assumed to be linearly homogeneous and twice differentiable. These are given below:

$$X_i = F_i(K_i^d, L_i) = L_i f_i(k_i^d) \quad (i = 2,3) \qquad (4.6)$$

$$X_N = F_N (L_N, \bar{K}_N^F) = L_N \, f_N \, (k_N^F) \tag{4.7}$$

Thus, the assumption of foreign capital specificity to one sector only has been restored.

Let p_i (3, N) denote the relative prices of commodity 3 and N, w the wage rate, π the rental on domestic capital and r_F the rental on foreign capital. Given the assumptions of perfect competition, profit maximization and that all commodities are produced it follows that the rewards to factors equal the value of their marginal products:

$$w = f_2 - k_2^d f_2' = p_3(f_3 - k_3^d f_3') = p_N(f_N - k_N^F f_N') \tag{4.8}$$

$$\pi = f_2' = p_3 \, f_3' \tag{4.9}$$

$$r_F = p_N f_N' \tag{4.10}$$

Factor endowments, domestic capital $(\bar{K}^d)$, domestic labour $(\bar{L})$ and foreign capital $(\bar{K}^F)$ are exogenously given and fully utilised so that:

$$k_2^d L_2 + k_3^d L_3 = \bar{K}^d \tag{4.11}$$

$$L_2 + L_3 + L_N = \bar{L} \tag{4.12}$$

$$k_N^F L_N = \bar{K}^F \tag{4.13}$$

Finally, the balance-of-payments equilibrium requires that:

$$E_2 = p_3 M_3 + r_F \, \bar{K}^F \tag{4.14}$$

In other words, the value of exports must equal the value of imports (which means imports of M_3 plus repatriation payments on foreign capital).

This completes the specification of the model. The system is closed by assuming that the terms of trade p_3 are given from outside.

4.2 Changes in Factor Endowments, Output Levels and Welfare

This section examines the consequences of a change in the total supply of primary factors domestic labour and foreign capital for: (a) output levels, and (b) welfare. To avoid repetition results regarding domestic capital accumulation will not be presented.

Consider first the impact of an exogenous change in the supply of labour assuming that accumulation occurs at constant terms of trade. However, in the present model it is not possible to hold the relative price of the non-traded good and the rental on foreign capital constant. This non-constancy occurs due to the income effect of factor accumulation which affects both the demand for the non-traded goods as well as the marginal product of foreign capital.

At constant terms of trade the capital intensity in sectors 2 and 3 cannot change (because a constant p_3 implies that the wage-domestic rental ratio is also constant). Hence the output changes in sectors 2 and 3 only depend on labour reallocation:

$$\frac{dX_2}{d\bar{L}} = f_2 \frac{dL_2}{d\bar{L}} \tag{4.15}$$

$$\frac{dX_3}{d\bar{L}} = f_3 . \frac{dL_3}{d\bar{L}} \tag{4.16}$$

From the factor endowment conditions it is known that:

$$\frac{dL_2}{d\bar{L}} = - \frac{k_3^d}{(k_2^d - k_3^d)} \left[1 - \frac{dL_N}{d\bar{L}} \right] \tag{4.17}$$

$$\frac{dL_3}{d\bar{L}} = \frac{k_2^d}{(k_2^d - k_3^d)} \left[1 - \frac{dL_N}{d\bar{L}} \right] \tag{4.18}$$

By using equation (4.16) and (4.17) it follows that:

$$\frac{dX_2}{d\bar{L}} = - \frac{k_3^d f_2}{(k_2^d - k_3^d)} \left[1 - \frac{dL_N}{d\bar{L}} \right] \qquad (4.19)$$

$$\frac{dX_3}{d\bar{L}} = \frac{k_2^d f_3}{(k_2^d - k_3^d)} \left[1 - \frac{dL_N}{d\bar{L}} \right] \qquad (4.20)$$

As previously remarked, it is not possible to hold the relative price of non-traded good constant and, therefore, the foreign capital intensity must change in the non-traded goods sector. Consequently, its output response depends on labour allocation as well as a change in the foreign capital intensity:

$$\frac{dX_N}{d\bar{L}} = f_N \frac{dL_N}{d\bar{L}} + L_N f'_N \frac{dk_N^F}{d\bar{L}}$$

which can be simplified to:

$$\frac{dX_N}{d\bar{L}} = \frac{w}{p_N} \frac{dL_N}{d\bar{L}} \qquad (4.21)$$

It is clear from equations (4.19) to (4.21) that the above output responses can only be interpreted when expresions have been obtained for $dL_N/d\bar{L}$. These can be obtained as follows. From equation (4.8) it is known that:

$$w = p_N (f_N - k_N^F f'_N)$$

Differentiating the above equation at a constant wage rate it follows that:

$$\frac{dk_N^F}{d\bar{L}} = \frac{f_N - k_N^F f'_N}{p_N k_N^F f''_N} \frac{dp_N}{d\bar{L}} \qquad (4.22)$$

It is also known from equation (4.5) that:

$$D_N (p_2, p_N, I) = X_N$$

where I denotes national income. It therefore follows that:

$$w \frac{dL_N}{d\bar{L}} = \frac{\partial D_N}{\partial p_N} \frac{dp_N}{d\bar{L}} + \frac{\partial D_N}{\partial I} \frac{dI}{dp_N} \qquad (4.23)$$

Following this it can easily be established that:

$$\frac{dL_N}{d\bar{L}} = - \frac{w\, L_N}{(k_N^F)^2\, f_N''} \frac{dp_N}{d\bar{L}} \qquad (4.24)$$

Then, substituting (4.24) into (4.23), and collecting terms, it follows that:

$$\frac{dp_N}{d\bar{L}} = - \frac{m_N}{B} \frac{dI}{d\bar{L}} \qquad (4.25)$$

where

$$B = \left[\frac{w^2\, L_N}{(k_N^F)^2\, f''_N} + \frac{\partial D_N}{\partial p_N} \right] < 0$$

To solve equation (4.25) a solution for the income change is needed. Using the method expounded in earlier chapters it is known that:

$$\frac{dI}{d\bar{L}} = \frac{1}{U_2} \frac{dU}{d\bar{L}} = w - \bar{K}^F \frac{dr_F}{d\bar{L}} \qquad (4.26)$$

By differentiating equations (4.10) and by suitable manipulation of terms it can be seen that:

$$\frac{dr_F}{d\bar{L}} = \frac{f_N}{k_N^F} \frac{dp_N}{d\bar{L}} \qquad (4.27)$$

71

Hence, by using (4.25) and (4.27) it follows:

$$\frac{dI}{d\bar{L}} = \frac{1}{U_2} \frac{dU}{d\bar{L}} = \frac{w}{A} \tag{4.28}$$

where

$$A = 1 - \frac{m_N \ f_N \ L_N}{B} > 0$$

It follows, therefore, that domestic labour accumulation always raises welfare.

Now, all of the required ingredients being available, it is possible to work backwards and obtain explicit solutions for all the variables. These are given below:[4]

$$\frac{dp_N}{d\bar{L}} = - \frac{m_N}{B} \frac{w}{A} > 0 \tag{4.29}$$

$$\frac{dr_F}{d\bar{L}} = \frac{f_N}{k_N^F} \frac{dp_N}{d\bar{L}} > 0 \tag{4.30}$$

$$\frac{dL_N}{d\bar{L}} = - \frac{w \ L_N}{(k_N^F)^2 \ f_N''} \frac{dp_N}{d\bar{L}} > 0 \tag{4.31}$$

$$\frac{dx_N}{d\bar{L}} = \frac{w}{p_N} \frac{dL_N}{d\bar{L}} > 0 \tag{4.32}$$

Since it is easy to show that $dL_N/d\bar{L} < 1$, it can be established that:

$$\frac{dx_2}{d\bar{L}} = - \frac{k_3^d \ f_2}{(k_2^d - k_3^d)} \left[1 - \frac{dL_N}{d\bar{L}} \right] \gtreqless 0 \text{ as } k_2^d - k_3^d \lesseqgtr 0 \tag{4.33}$$

$$\frac{dX_3}{d\bar{L}} = \frac{k_2^d f_3}{(k_2^d - k_3^d)} \left[1 - \frac{dL_N}{d\bar{L}} \right] \gtrless 0 \quad \text{as} \quad k_2^d - k_3^d \gtrless 0 \quad (4.34)$$

The above output responses are the same as predicted by the well known Rybczynski theorem.

The presentation of all of the consequences of labour accumulation has now been completed. Consequently, it is time to provide an explanation of the results which were described above in an intuitive manner. This can best be achieved with the use of box diagram 4.1. There are three factors of production in the model all with inelastic supply: labour $(\bar{L})$, domestic capital $(\bar{K}^d)$ and the specific factor, foreign capital $(\bar{K}^F)$. However, sector N uses only labour $(\bar{L})$ and the specific factor $(\bar{K}^F)$. Since both these factors of production are in fixed supply a box can be constructed as in the lower half of Figure 4.1. The dimensions of this box $O_N K^F K'^F L$ represent the total supply of the factors of production labour and the specific factor. The vertical distance $O_N K^F$ (and $L K'^F$) represent the supply of the specific factor $(\bar{K}^F)$; and the horizontal line $O_N L$ (and $K^F K'^F$) the supply of labour. Output of commodity N is measured by reference to origin O_N. Also note that to keep the specific factor fully employed the output of sector N must prevail on line $K^F K'^F$.

Suppose the output of the non-traded good X_N is fixed at the level $O_N O_N'$ where the isoquant $x_N x_N$ is tangential to the wage-foreign rental ratio (w/r_F). This implies that the non-traded goods sector uses $O_N L_N$ of labour and the total supply of the specific factor $\bar{K}^F$ $(O_N K^F)$. The remaining supply of labour $(\bar{L} - L_N)$ denoted by $L_N L$ along with domestic capital can be used for producing commodities X_2 and X_3. From points O_N' and K'^F another box can be constructed with the dimensions representing the domestic capital and labour available for sectors 2 and 3. This box is given by $O_N' K^d O_2 K'^F$. The supply of domestic capital is indicated by $O_N' K^d$ (and $O_2 K'^F$) and that of labour available for use in sectors 2 and 3 by $O_N' K'^F$ (and $K^d O_2$). Let O_N' be the origin for isoquants of sector 3 and O_2 for sector 2. A contract curve can then be traced between the origins $O_N' O_2$ (not shown). Suppose production occurs at point D where the isoquants of sectors 2 and 3 are tangential to the wage rental on domestic capital ratio (w/π). This then completes the

Figure 4.1

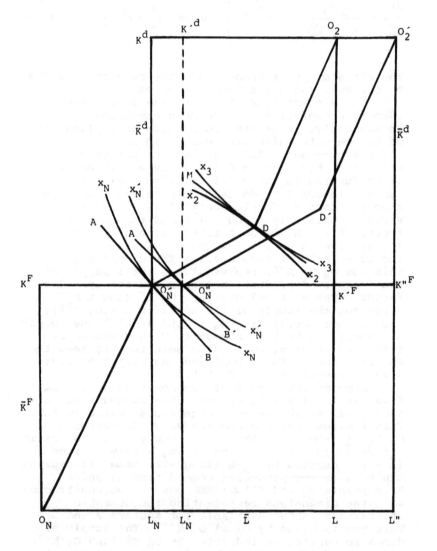

description of an equilibrium situation in the model
which has been established.

Now, however, suppose that the labour available
to the economy increases from O_N L to O_N L" - that
is, the lower box now becomes O_N K^F K "F L". From
equation (4.31) it is clear that sector N now uses
more labour, therefore, the output equilibrium for
sector N must lie to the right of point O_N^- (and its
output must rise as shown by equation (4.32)).
Suppose this occurs at point $O_N^"$ where the isoquant
$x_N^- x_N^-$ is tangential to the wage rental on foreign
capital ratio (w/r_F)(note this is different from
w/π). It is clear that the factor price line A´B´
is flatter than A B which implies that r_F must rise
both relatively and absolutely because w is fixed by
the constant terms of trade (a result shown by
equation (4.30)). This occurs because the same
amount of capital is used more intensively and,
given perfect competition, this also implies a rise
in p_N. The box for domestic capital and the supply
of labour available to sectors 2 and 3 now becomes
$O_N^"$ K "F O_2^- K^-d. The new equilibrium at constant
prices occurs at point D´ which indicates an
increase in the output of the labour-intensive
sector X_3 and a decline in the output of the
domestic capital-intensive sector X_2.

The implications of foreign capital accumulation can be derived by using the same procedure as
the one used for labour accumulation. The main
results are summarised below:

$$\frac{dp_N}{d\bar{K}^F} = A \bar{K}^F L_N f_N \left[\frac{m_N L_N f_N}{A + L_N f_N m_N} - 1 \right] < 0 \quad (4.35)$$

$$\frac{dr_F}{d\bar{K}^F} = \frac{f_N}{\bar{K}_N^F} \frac{dp_N}{d\bar{K}^F} < 0 \quad (4.36)$$

$$\frac{1}{U_2} \frac{dU}{d\bar{K}^F} = - L_N f_N \frac{dp_N}{d\bar{K}^F} > 0 \quad (4.37)$$

Some comments can be made with respect to equations
(4.34) to (4.36). It is clear that foreign capital
accumulation leads to an increase in national

welfare in spite of the presence of monopoly power
in trade of capital. This result stands in sharp
contrast to previous propositions which show that an
increase in foreign capital leaves welfare unchanged.
This change occurs because of the relaxation of the
condition that, given the terms of trade, all prices
are fixed. In the present model all prices are not
constant when foreign capital accumulation occurs,
which causes a change in both the relative price of
the non-traded good as well as the return on foreign
capital. Only the terms of trade are held constant
when factor accumulation occurs.

The intuitive explanation of an increase in
welfare as a consequence of foreign capital accumulation is easily developed by examining equations
(4.35) to (4.37). It is clear from these equations
that both the relative price of a non-traded good
and the return on foreign capital fall as a result
of foreign capital accumulation. Lowering the
return on foreign capital also lowers the burden of
repatriation payments for the home country, and
therefore welfare rises.

The output movements in the non-traded goods
sector depends on price and income change. However,
in the traded goods sectors these depend on labour
allocation at constant prices and are in accord with
Rybczynski theorem. These output movements are
presented diagrammatically in Figure 4.2. The
diagram is self explanatory.

4.3 Commodity Prices and Factor Rentals

This section analyses the impact of a change in the
commodity prices on real factor rewards. In order
to simplify the presentation of results, it will be
assumed that the marginal product of labour and
foreign capital are constant in the non-traded goods
sector. This implies that $f_N'' = 0$. This particular
condition does not lead to any serious loss of
generality in the qualitative nature of results, but
it does help to present several results in such a
simple manner that the class conflict can be seen
more easily. Suppose that the relative price of
importables p_3 increases (this is equivalent to
imposing a tariff). An increase in this price has
an impact on the relative price of the non-traded
good p_N, the wage rate w, the rental on domestic
capital π and the return to the specific factor
foreign capital r_F. From the factor market
equilibrium conditions it follows that:

Figure 4.2

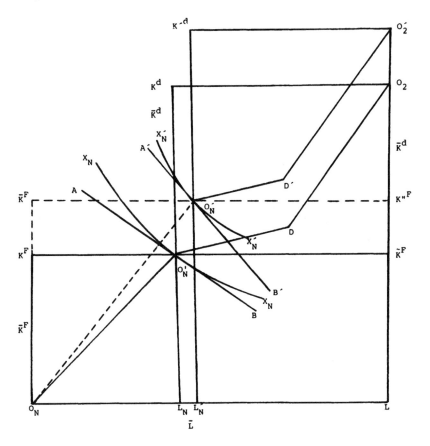

$$\frac{dw}{dp_3} = k_2^d \, f_2'' \, \frac{dk_2^d}{dp_3} \qquad (4.38)$$

$$\frac{d\pi}{dp_3} = f_2'' \, \frac{dk_2^d}{dp_3} \qquad (4.39)$$

$$\frac{dr_F}{dp_3} = f_N' \, \frac{dp_N}{dp_3} \qquad (4.40)$$

The Solution for dk_2^d/dp_3 and dp_N/dp_3 (given the assumption that $f_N'' = 0$) can be obtained from the marginal productivity conditions. Having obtained them and by substituting in equations (4.37) to (4.39) it follows:

$$\frac{1}{w} \frac{dw}{dp_3} = - \frac{k_2^d \, f_3}{w(k_3^d - k_2^d)} \qquad (4.41)$$

$$\frac{1}{\pi} \frac{d\pi}{dp_3} = \frac{w + \pi \, k_3^d}{\pi \, (k_3^d - k_2^d)} \qquad (4.42)$$

$$\frac{1}{r_F} \frac{dr_F}{dp_3} = - \frac{k_2^d \, f_3}{w \, (k_3^d - k_2^d)} \qquad (4.43)$$

$$\frac{1}{p_N} \frac{dp_N}{dp_3} = - \frac{k_2^d \, f_3}{w(k_3^d - k_2^d)} \qquad (4.44)$$

Several interesting results emerge from equations (4.41) to (4.44). First, it is clear from equations (4.41), (4.43) and (4.44) that w, r_F and p_N have a sign opposite to that of:

$$(k_3^d - k_2^d)$$

and π has the same sign as:

$$(k_3^d - k_2^d).$$

In other words, the real wage rate, the return to foreign capital and the relative price of non-traded good all rise when importables are labour-intensive:

$$(k_3^d < k_2^d)$$

and all fall when importables are capital-intensive. The rental on domestic capital increases (decreases) when importables are capital (labour) intensive. Second, it is clear from equations (4.41), (4.43) and (4.44) that the wage rate w, the rental on foreign capital r_F and the relative price of the non-traded good p_N, rises or falls by exactly the same magnitude - a consequence of the assumption of constancy of marginal product in sector N. Third, since p_3 is the relative price of the importable good it follows that the demand for protection will be characterized by the following group alignments.

Case I: $k_3^d > k_2^d$ (Importable sector capital-
                            Intensive)

(i) Protection will be favoured by owners of capital because $(1/\pi)\ (d\pi/dp_3) > 0$.

(ii) Protection will be opposed by labour because $(1/w)\ (dw/dp_3) < 0$, and owners of foreign capital $(1/r_F)\ (dr_F/dp_3) < 0$.

Case II: $k_2^d > k_3^d$ (Importable sector labour-
                            Intensive)

(i) Protection will be favoured by labour $(1/w)$ $(dw/dp_3) > 0$, and by owners of foreign capital $(1/r_F)\ (dr_F/dp_3) > 0$.

(ii) Protection will be opposed by owners of domestic capital $(1/\pi)\ (d\pi/dp_3) < 0$.

It is clear from the above discussion that the demand for protection is not necessarily a two class problem, namely a clash of interest between capitalists and workers. Moreover, labour and foreign capitalists need not be in direct conflict with each other - in fact they might agree to become

79

"strange bed fellows".

4.4 Conclusions

This chapter clearly demonstrates the role of
specificity in the non-traded goods sector. Three
major results emerge from this investigation. First,
it is not, in general, possible to generate several
trade results on the basis of fix price assumption so
often used in trade theory literature. The relaxation of this fix price assumption shows that
domestic factor accumulation raises the reward of
foreign-owned capital used in the non-traded goods
sector. Thus the foreigners have a vested interest
in promoting growth via the accumulation of domestic
factors. Second, in sharp contrast to results of
previous chapters foreign capital accumulation raises
welfare in spite of the presence of uncorrected
monopoly power in trade of capital. This is because
of income and price effects of foreign capital
specificity in the non-traded goods sector. Finally,
labour and foreign capitalists can become "strange
bed fellows" in terms of demand for protection.

NOTES

1.   The role of specific factors in trade theory
has been examined by several authors, see for
example Fishburn and Kemp (2), Hazari and Pattanaik
(6), Jones (8) and Mussa (11).
2.   An elaborate treatment of this model is
available in Hazari-Sgro-Suh (5) and Komiya (7).
3.   This type of specificity without foreign
ownership of capital has been explored by Hazari (4).
4.   This result is surprising in the context of
trade and distortion theory, but not in the context
of distortion theory with factor specificity, see
for example Hazari and Pattanaik (6).

REFERENCES

(1) Corden, W.M. and Gruen, F.H. 1970. A Tariff That
    Worsens the Terms of Trade. In I. McDougall and
    R. Snape (ed.), *Studies in International Economics
    Economics*. Amsterdam, North Holland.
(2) Fishburn, G. and Kemp, M.C. 1977. An Analysis of
    Price: Rental and Endowment: Output Relationships
    in Terms of Specific Factors and Product Blocks.
    Economic Record, Vol.53 (June-September)219-26.
(3) Hazari, B.R. 1977. Factor Accumulation, Terms
    of Trade and Welfare in a Three Commodity, Three

Factor Model of International Trade. *Australian
Economic Papers*, Vol.17 (December) 267-72.

(4) Hazari, B.R. On Specific Factors in the Non-
Traded Goods Sector and Some Propositions in The
Pure Theory of International Trade. Forthcoming:
Greek Economic Review.

(5) Hazari, B.R. and Pattanaik, P.K. 1980. Some
Welfare Propositions in a Three Commodity, Three
Factor Model of Trade. *Greek Economic Review*,
Vol.2 (April) 12-23.

(6) Hazari, B.R., Sgro, P.M. and Suh, D.C. 1981.
*Non-Traded and Intermediate Goods and the Pure
Theory of International Trade*. London: Croom
Helm.

(7) Komiya, R. 1967. Non-Traded Goods and the Pure
Theory of International Trade. *International
Economic Review*, Vol.8 (June) 132-52.

(8) Jones, R.W. 1975. Income Distribution and
Effective Protection in a Multi-Commodity Trade
Model. *Journal of Economic Theory*, Vol.11
(August) 1-15.

(9) Mayer, W. 1974. Short-run and Long-run
Equilibrium for a Small Open Economy. *Journal of
Political Economy*, Vol.82 (September-October)
955-68.

(10) Melvin, J.R. 1968. Production and Trade with
Two Factors and Three Goods. *American Economic
Review*, Vol.58 (December) 1240-68.

(11) Mussa, M. 1974. Tariffs and the Distribution of
Income: The Importance of Factor Specificity,
Substitutability and Intensity in the Short and
Long-Run. *Journal of Political Economy*, Vol.82
(November-December) 1191-03.

Chapter 5

ON EMPLOYMENT AND THE WELFARE EFFECT OF FOREIGN
CAPITAL ACCUMULATION IN A MINIMUM WAGE MODEL OF
AN OPEN ECONOMY

This chapter is concerned with providing an example
in which increased inflow of foreign capital not
only lowers the level of employment (increases
unemployment), but also lowers national welfare, in
the presence of a real minimum wage above the
competitive level. It is known that the imposition
of a real wage rate above the competitive level
generally results in unemployment being created.
This employment displacement effect of the imposition
of a real wage has been noted by several authors in
the context of trade theory.[1] However, it has not
been the subject of investigation in the context of
partial mobility and foreign ownership of capital.[2]
The result that foreign capital accumulation may
lower both employment and welfare casts serious
doubts on the frequently cited hypothesis that such
accumulation raises both employment and welfare. In
the standard two-commodity, two-factor model of
international trade the employment benefit of capital
accumulation is not destroyed by the presence of a
minimum real wage constraint (although the welfare
effects of such accumulation are ambiguous).
However, in a model consisting of more than two-
factors and two-commodities capital accumulation may
lower both welfare and employment. The object of
this chapter is to provide a counter-example to this
commonly held belief, and a very simple model is all
that is required.

5.1 The Model

In order to produce the result that an increased
inflow of foreign capital may lower employment
(increase unemployment) and welfare, the model of
Chapter 3 needs to be extended. Another totally
mobile factor land is now included in the analysis.

82

To obtain unemployment in the system, a real minimum wage constraint (binding on the entire production surface) is also introduced. To avoid repetition, the only equations produced below are those which are amended due to the introduction of the above changes.

The production functions of Chapter 3 now become:

$$X_1 = F_1 \; (L_1, \; T_1, \; K_1^d) \tag{5.1}$$

$$X_2 = F_2 \; (L_2, \; T_2, \; K_2^F) \tag{5.2}$$

$$X_3 = F_3 \; (L_3, \; T_3, \; K_3^d) \tag{5.3}$$

$$X_N = F_N \; (L_N, \; T_N, \; K_N^F) \tag{5.4}$$

In the above production functions (in contrast with those of Chapter 3) the factor land (T) has been introduced and its allocation to various sectors is denoted by T_i (i = 1,2,3,N). All the restrictions imposed on the production functions in Chapter 3 also apply to the above production functions.

The country is again assumed to be small so that the price of traded goods is given exogenously. A binding minimum wage is defined in terms of commodity 1, so that:

$$w_1 = \bar{w} \tag{5.5}$$

where $\bar{w}$ is the institutionally determined real wage rate in terms of commodity 1 that applies to the entire economy. This minimum wage will be assumed to be above the competitive level and determined exogenously (for instance by government or the trade unions).

The factor endowment conditions now become:

$$a_{L1} X_1 + a_{L2} X_2 + a_{L3} X_3 + a_{LN} X_N = L_a < \bar{L} \tag{5.6}$$

$$a_{K1}^d X_1 \qquad + a_{K3}^d X_3 \qquad = \bar{K}^d \tag{5.7}$$

$$a_{K2}^F X_2 \qquad + a_{KN}^F X_N = \bar{K}_N^F \tag{5.8}$$

$$a_{T1} X_1 + a_{T2} X_2 + a_{T3} X_3 + a_{TN} X_N = \bar{T} \qquad (5.9)$$

In equation (5.6) L_a denotes the actual level of employment which is less than the total endowment of labour $\bar{L}$. Therefore, part of the labour force, due to the binding minimum wage constraint, is unemployed. Now by using minimum wage constraint coupled with the given terms of trade and the relevant equations from Chapter 3 the system can be solved uniquely for all a_{ij}s. These a_{ij}s cannot change unless prices are allowed to vary. The system can be completed by using the remaining and relevant equations from Chapter 3.

5.2 Effects of An Increase in Foreign Factor Accumulation

The possibility that foreign capital accumulation may lower both welfare and employment in the presence of a minimum wage constraint can now be established. Recall that national income from the factor side is given by:

$$I = \bar{w} L_a + \pi \bar{K}^d + \bar{\pi} \bar{T} \qquad (5.10)$$

where L_a denotes the actual level of employment, $\bar{w}$ the fixed real wage, π the rental on domestic capital and $\bar{\pi}$ the rent on land. By differentiating equation (5.10) at constant prices with respect to $\bar{K}^F$ it can be seen that:

$$\frac{dI}{d\bar{K}^F} = \bar{w} \frac{dL_a}{d\bar{K}^F} \qquad (5.11)$$

The above equation shows that the change in national income (welfare) depends on the response of the actual labour force employed to the change in the stock of foreign capital. If the level of employment falls (rises) then immiserizing (normal) growth follows. Of course, in the model without the minimum wage rate :

$$dL_a/d\bar{K}^F$$

is equal to zero and the result reported earlier in

this work follows, i.e. $dI/d\bar{K}^F = 0$.

From the equilibrium condition for the non-traded goods market it is known that $D_N = X_N$, hence:

$$\frac{dX_N}{d\bar{K}^F} = \eta_N \frac{dI}{d\bar{K}^F} = m_N \bar{w} \frac{dL_a}{d\bar{K}^F} \qquad (5.12)$$

Prices have again been assumed to be constant. The term m_N denotes the marginal propensity to consume the non-traded good and its value lies between 0 and 1 $(0 < m_N < 1)$.

By differentiating equations (5.6) to (5.9) and using (5.11) the following expressions (at constant prices) are obtained:

$$a_{L1} \frac{dX_1}{d\bar{K}^F} + a_{L2} \frac{dX_2}{d\bar{K}^F} + a_{L3} \frac{dX_3}{d\bar{K}^F} + (a_{LN} \bar{w} m_N - 1) \frac{dL_a}{d\bar{K}^F} = 0 \qquad (5.13)$$

$$a_{K1}^d \frac{dX_1}{d\bar{K}^F} + a_{K3}^d \frac{dX_3}{d\bar{K}^F} = 0 \qquad (5.14)$$

$$a_{K2}^F \frac{dX_2}{d\bar{K}^F} + a_{KN}^F \bar{w} m_N \frac{dL_a}{d\bar{K}^F} = 1 \qquad (5.15)$$

$$a_{T1} \frac{dX_1}{d\bar{K}^F} + a_{T2} \frac{dX_2}{d\bar{K}^F} + a_{T3} \frac{dX_3}{d\bar{K}^F} + a_{TN} \bar{w} m_N \frac{dL_a}{d\bar{K}^F} = 0 \qquad (5.16)$$

The above system gives four equations in four unknowns. Here the only interest is with the response of employment to foreign capital accumulation. This can be obtained by solving for $dL_a/d\bar{K}^F$, and the solution is given below:

$$\frac{dL_a}{d\bar{K}^F} = \frac{A(k_{1T}^d - k_{3T}^d) - B(k_{1L}^d - k_{3L}^d)}{\bar{w} m_N C(k_{2T}^F - k_{NT}^F)(k_{1L}^d - k_{3L}^d) + \bar{w} m_N (D(k_{NL}^F - k_{2F}^L) + E)(k_{1T}^d - k_{3T}^d)}$$

$$(5.17)$$

where

$$A = a_{L2}\, a_{T1}\, a_{T3} \qquad > 0$$

$$B = a_{T2}\, a_{L1}\, a_{L3} \qquad > 0$$

$$C = a_{T2}\, a_{TN}\, a_{L1} \qquad > 0$$

$$D = a_{L2}\, a_{LN}\, a_{T1}\, a_{T3} > 0$$

$$E = a_{K2}^{F}\, a_{T1}\, a_{T3} \qquad > 0$$

k_{1T}^{d} = Sector 1 domestic-capital-land ratio

k_{3T}^{d} = Sector 3 domestic-capital-land ratio

k_{1L}^{d} = Sector 1 domestic-capital-labour ratio

k_{3L}^{d} = Sector 3 domestic-capital-labour ratio

k_{2T}^{F} = Sector 3 foreign capital-land ratio

k_{NT}^{F} = Sector N foreign capital-land ratio

k_{NL}^{F} = Sector N foreign capital-labour ratio

k_{2L}^{F} = Sector 2 foreign capital-labour ratio

The remaining task is to interpret equation (5.17). Suppose the following relations hold regarding factor intensities:

$$k_{2T}^{F} > k_{NT}^{F}$$

$$k_{NL}^{F} > k_{2F}^{L}$$

$$k_{1L}^{d} > k_{3L}^{d}$$

$$k_{1T}^{d} > k_{3T}^{d}$$

Given the above restrictions it is clear that the denominator of equation (5.16) is positive. The sign of the numerator depends on:

$$A(k_{1T}^{d} - k_{3T}^{d}) - B(k_{1L}^{d} - k_{3L}^{d}).$$

The first term is positive while the second negative.

Therefore, it follows that (for the above intensities):

$$\frac{dL_a}{d\bar{K}^F} < 0 \text{ if and only if } A(k^d_{1T} - k^d_{3T}) - B(k^d_{1L} - k^d_{3L}) < 0 \quad (5.18)$$

It is also clear from equation (5.11) that if unemployment increases:

$$(dL_a/d\bar{K}^F < 0)$$

then welfare also decreases:

$$(dI/d\bar{K}^F < 0)$$

An intuitive explanation of the above result runs along the following lines. It is obvious that if income falls, i.e.:

$$dI/d\bar{K}^F < 0$$

then the output of the non-traded goods sector must decline:

$$(dX_N/d\bar{K}^F = m_N \ dI/d\bar{K}^F).$$

Note that the non-traded goods sector is foreign capital-labour intensive:

$$(k^N_{FL} > k^F_{2L})$$

and sector 2 is foreign capital-land intensive:

$$(k^F_{2T} > k^F_{NT}).$$

Therefore, when the output of the non-traded goods sector declines it releases foreign capital in a proportion greater than labour and less than land. Hence in order to maintain the full utilisation of foreign capital the total labour employed by sectors 2 and N must fall. It is not essential for the other sectors to absorb the redundant labour force. They could adjust without using additional labour force according to the Rybczynski theorem.

It has now successfully been shown that an increase in foreign capital may not only increase unemployment, but also result in immiserizing growth". The traditional belief that there are employment benefits associated with foreign inflow of capital should be taken with a large rather than a small pinch of salt!

NOTES

1. See for example Brecher (1), Hazari (3), (4) and Sgro (5).
2. The exception to this remark is a note by Brecher (2).

REFERENCES

(1) Brecher, R.A. 1971. *Minimum Wage Rate and the Pure Theory of International Trade*. Unpublished PhD Thesis, Havard University.
(2) ———— 1981. Increased Unemployment From Capital Accumulation in a Minimum Wage Model of An Open Economy. *Canadian Journal of Economics*, Vol.13 (December) 152-58.
(3) Hazari, B.R. 1974. Factor Market Distortions And Gains From Trade Revisited. *Weltwirtschafliches Archiv*, Vol.110 (October) 413-29.
(4) ———— 1978. *The Pure Theory of International Trade and Distortions*. London: Croom Helm.
(5) Sgro, P.M. 1980. *Wage Differentials and Economic Growth*. London: Croom Helm.

Chapter 6

INDENTURED LABOUR AND ITS EXPLOITATION IN A
NEOCLASSICAL MODEL OF INTERNATIONAL TRADE

The object of this chapter is to incorporate the
presence and exploitation of indentured labour in a
neoclassical model of international trade. Interest
in modelling this problem arose out of reading
several interesting pieces of work about the social
origins, recruitment procedures and the sorry plight
of indentured labourers on the plantations,
specially in Fiji. This country received nearly
60,000 Indians as indentured labourers in the period
1879 to 1916.[1] Although many books and papers have
been written about these workers, no attempt appears
to have been made to construct a model of a small
open economy that incorporates 'Girmit' labour.[2]
Hopefully, the following observations may help to
obviate this lacuna in the literature.
     Before proceeding to set up a model it is
important to comment upon the exploitaiton of
indentured labour. The existing literature which
deals with this type of labour indicates that this
is a hotly disputed issue - some authors assert that
the indentured labour was exploited whilst others
aver that no such exploitation occurred. The two
quotations given below illustrate this point. The
Sanderson Committee in 1910 upheld the view that
exploitation did not occur:

> It may be confidently stated that as a general
> rule the immigrants in all the colonies to
> which they go improve in health, strength and
> independence of character. These results, even
> though they affect only a fractional proportion
> of the vast population of India, cannot be
> regarded otherwise than with satisfaction.[3]

The two following quotations, on the other hand,
support the contention that indentured labour was

exploited on the plantation. Miss Dudley made the
following observations: [4]

> They arrive in this country timid, fearful
> women, not knowing where they are to be sent.
> They are alloted to plantations like so many
> dumb animals. If they do not perform
> satisfactorily the work given them, they are
> struck or fined, or they are even sent to gaol.
> The life of the plantations alters their
> demeanour and even their very faces. Some
> look crushed and broken-hearted, others sullen,
> others hard and evil. I shall never forget
> the first time I saw 'identured' women when
> they were returning from their day's work.
> The look on those women's faces haunts me.

In a report by the Sergeant of Police at Labasa to
his Superintendent in Suva in 1897 observed: [5]

> Sergt. Mason begs to inform the Supt. that it
> is a usual thing for Indians to come to the
> Police Station between the hours of 9 and 12 at
> night to complain of the treatment they get on
> some of the plantations and when asked why they
> are so late they say that they have to wait
> till dark as the Sirdahs watch them and will not
> let them go. This is when they have been
> beaten during the day and if the overseers hear
> that they have been to the Police Station they
> get another thrashing. Directly the overseer
> hears that the Sirdah has beaten any of the
> people he at once caution the one who got the
> beating and all who saw it that if they go to
> complain to the S.M. or Sergt. that he will
> beat them and give them heavy work to do. The
> consequence is that when any of the people are
> ill used they cannot get any of those who saw
> it to go as witness for them because of these
> threats.

More evidence can be cited in support of both
viewpoints about exploitation. However, after
reading the material on this subject, it is reasonable to contend that indentured labour was in fact
exploited. But the intriguing aspect is whether it
is possible to explain the nature of such exploitation on the basis of a meaningful economic model.
The following is an attempt to produce such a model.

6.1 A Model of Exploitation of Indentured Labour

Consider an economy in which four commodities are produced, X_1, X_2, X_3 and X_4. Commodities X_3 and X_4 are produced with the help of domestic labour and domestic capital; while commodity X_1 is produced with the aid of foreign capital and domestic labour. The production functions for these sectors X_1, X_3, X_4 are assumed to exhibit constant returns to scale and diminishing returns along the isoquants:

$$X_1 = F_1 \ (K_1^F, \ L_1) = L_1 \ f_1 \ (k_1^F) \qquad (6.1)$$

$$X_3 = F_3 \ (K_3^d, \ L_3) = L_3 \ f_3 \ (k_3^d) \qquad (6.2)$$

$$X_4 = F_4 \ (K_4^d, \ L_4) = L_4 \ f_4 \ (k_4^d) \qquad (6.3)$$

where

$$K_i^d, \ L_i \ (i = 3)$$

indicate the allocation of domestic labour and domestic capital to sectors 3 and 4 and

$$k_i^d \ (i = 3,4)$$

the domestic-capital-labour ratios. The values of K_1^F and L_1 show the allocation of foreign capital and domestic labour to sector 1 and k_1^F the foreign capital-domestic labour ratio.

Output of sector 2 is produced with the help of foreign capital and indentured labour. The production function for sector 2 is assumed to exhibit constant returns to scale as well as constant returns to factors. This production function is given below:

$$X_2 = F_2 \ (K_2^F, \ \bar{H}^I) = \bar{H}^I \ f_2 \ (k_2^F) \qquad (6.4)$$

The term K_2^F shows the allocation of foreign capital to sector 2. Indentured labour is used as a specific factor by sector 2 and is written in terms of number of hours which are denoted by $\bar{H}^I$. Two observations are in order regarding the above

production function. First, it is assumed that the
indentured labour is sector specific. This is not
an unrealistic assumption since in Fiji most of the
indentured labour was throughout utilised on sugar
plantations. The use of indentured labour in other
sectors was negligible. Second, the production
function has been written in terms of the specific
number of hours the workers worked. This is so
because the indentured labour was assigned tasks and
the hours were increased arbitrarily whenever the
work was not completed. Number of hours of work
were also increased for other reasons, therefore, it
makes sense to write sector 2's production function
in terms of fixed number of hours, $\bar{H}^I$.

6.1a Wage Determination in Sector 2

In an exceedingly important paper Akerlof (1)
examined the consequences of asymmetrical distribution of information between buyers and sellers and
he arrived at certain conclusions regarding the
market for lemons (second-hand cars). The
conceptual framework of Akerlof's paper is equally
applicable to the wage determination process of
indentured labour. Although an explicit model for
this wage determination will not be set up in this
chapter,[6] the Akerlofian framework can be drawn upon
to make some observations regarding the wages paid
to indentured labour. These remarks are in the
context of the Fijian economy in the nineteenth
century.
     Indentured labourers were recruited from India
and brought to Fiji. These labourers were offered a
contract which they appear to have signed volunt-
arily. However, the information sets of those
recruiting and those signing the contracts were not
the same. The recruiting agencies and colonial
bureaucracy had much more access to information than
those becoming indentured labourers. This
asymmetrical distribution can be said to have led to
a payment of wage rates to indentured labourers
below the value of their marginal product.
     The indentured labourers recruited from India
invariably compared the wage offered in the
contracts with their earnings in India. Thus, as
far as these workers were concerned the recruiters
were offering them a wage greater than they would
have expected in India.[7] If this wage was lower than
that which had to be paid to workers in Fiji (either
local or imported from other islands), then there
was an element of surplus[8] (pure profit)

for the planters using the cheap labour force from India.[9] The abject poverty that prevailed in India is beautifully brought out by the following passages of poetry. These passages are taken from the important work of Lal (5) on Indian indentured labour in Fiji:[10]

> From the east came the rail, from the west
>   came the ship,
> And took my beloved one away.
> The rail has become my sawat,
> Which took my beloved one away.
> The rail is not my enemy, for the ship,
> O! It is money which is the real enemy.
> It takes my beloved one from place to place,
> Money is the enemy...
>
> Mother! Far away in a distant land,
> The thought of thine is crushing me
> Poverty, abject poverty, mother,
> Has separated me from thee.

The deception involved in not telling the true conditions in colonies is also well brought out in poetry and prose. This can be seen from the following passages of poetry from Lal's thesis (6):

> Oh recruiter, your heart is deceitful,
> Your speech is full of lies.
> Tender may be your voice, articulate and
>   seemingly logical,
> But it is all used to defame and destroy
> The good names of people.
>
> I hoe all day and cannot sleep at night,
> Today my whole body aches
> Damnation to you, arkatis.
>
> O! Registration Officers,
> May death befall you:
> You have deprived me of my marriage bed.
>
> Several months on the ship passed with
>   great difficulty,
> On the seven dark seas,
>   we suffered unaccustomed problems.
>
> The six foot by eight foot CSR room
> Is the source of all comfort for us.
> In it we keep our tools and hoe,
> And also the grinding stove and the hearth.

In it is also kept the firewood.
It is our single and double-storey palace,
In which is made our golden parapet.

Having provided evidence with regard to the
assertion that the information sets of buyers and
sellers were not equal,[11] the next task is to give
meaning to the term "exploitation". This latter
term will be taken to mean a payment to workers that
was less than the value of their marginal product.
Thus, the wage, w^I, paid to the indentured labour:

$$w^I = \alpha \, p_2 \, (f_2 - k_2^F \, f_2') \qquad 0 < \alpha < 1 \qquad (6.5)$$

where α represents the degree of exploitation. The
value of α close to zero represents a large gap
between the value of the marginal product and the
wage actually paid, while α equal to 1 represents
equality between the wage rate and the value of
marginal product. The latter case represents no
exploitation.

The value of α is endogenously determined and
is taken to be a function of the number of hours
worked:

$$\alpha = g \, (\bar{H}^I) \qquad g' < 0 \qquad (6.6)$$

The surplus (pure profit) earned by the planters is
now given by:

$$S = (1 - \alpha) \, p_2 \, (f_2 - k_2^F \, f_2') \qquad (6.7)$$

This may be termed the exploitation function. It is
important to note that exploitation in the above
system arises due to imperfections in the market
structure. This should be clearly distinguished
from the notion of exploitation in a Marxian framework in which it is defined in terms of surplus
value. The Marxian definition does not involve any
notion of market imperfection for defining exploitation.

6.1b Rest of the Model

The rest of the model is set out below. The
aggregate utility function is given by:

$$U = U(D_1, D_2, D_3, D_4) \qquad (6.8)$$

94

where D_i $(i = 1...4)$ represents the domestic consumption of the four commodities. The utility function is assumed to satisfy the restrictions already imposed in earlier chapters.

The first order equilibrium conditions again require that:

$$\frac{U_1}{P_1} = \frac{U_2}{P_2} = \frac{U_3}{P_3} = \frac{U_4}{P_4} \qquad (6.9)$$

The above equation can be interpreted along the same lines as the corresponding equation in the previous chapters.

It is assumed that commodities 1 and 2 are exported, and 3 and 4 are imported so that:

$$D_1 = X_1 - E_1 \qquad (6.10)$$

$$D_2 = X_2 - E_2 \qquad (6.11)$$

$$D_3 = X_3 + M_3 \qquad (6.12)$$

$$D_4 = X_4 + M_4 \qquad (6.13)$$

The meaning of these equations by now should be fairly obvious.

Competitive conditions prevail in the market for labour, foreign capital and domestic capital. Given this assumption along with incomplete specialization and profit maximization the usual conditions regarding factor rewards follow:

$$w = p_1 \ (f_1 - k_1^F \ f_1') = p_3 \ (f_3 - k_3^d \ f_3') = p_4 \ (f_4 - k_4^d \ f_4') \qquad (6.14)$$

$$r_F = p_1 \ f_1' = p_2 \ f_2' \qquad (6.15)$$

$$\pi = p_3 \ f_3' = p_4 \ f_4' \qquad (6.16)$$

To keep the analysis as simple as possible, it can be assumed that both the earnings on foreign capital and the surplus generated from exploiting labour are exported, so that the balance-of-payments equilibrium requires :

$$p_1 E_1 + p_2 E_2 = p_3 M_3 + p_4 M_4 + r_F \ \bar{K}^F + S\bar{H}^I \qquad (6.17)$$

95

The above equation shows that the value of exports equals the value of imports plus repatriation payments.

Finally, full employment conditions require that:

$$L_1 \, k_1^F + \bar{H}^I \, k_2^F = \bar{K}^F \tag{6.18}$$

$$L_1 + L_3 + L_4 = \bar{L} \tag{6.19}$$

$$k_3^d \, L_3 + k_4^d \, L_4 = \bar{K}^d \tag{6.20}$$

This completes the specification of the model. The system consists of the fcllowing unknowns:

$$U, \; D_1, \; D_2, \; D_3, \; D_4, \; P_1, \; P_2, \; P_3, \; P_4, \; X_1, \; E_1, \; X_2,$$
$$E_2, \; X_3, \; M_3, \; X_4, \; M_4, \; K_1^F, \; L_1, \; k_1^F, \; k_2^F, \; k_3^d, \; L_3, K_2^F,$$
$$k_3^d, \; k_4^d, \; L_4, \; k_4^d, \; \alpha, \; w^I, \; w, \; r_F, \; \pi \text{ and } S$$

that is, a system of thirty-four unknowns in thirty equations. The system is closed by making the small country assumption.

6.2 Results

In this section the results relating to parametric variation in only one variable on exploitation and welfare are presented. This parametric change concerns the number of hours worked by indentured labour. The reader can work out the impact of other parametric variations quite easily on the basis of the model presented.

Consider the impact of a change in the number of hours worked (by indentured labour) both on welfare and the surplus generated. By differentiating the utility function at constant prices and using techniques outlined earlier, the following result can be obtained:

$$\frac{1}{U_1} \frac{dU}{d\bar{H}^I} = \frac{dX_1}{d\bar{H}^I} + \frac{P_2}{P_1} \frac{dX_2}{d\bar{H}^I} + \frac{P_3}{P_1} \frac{dX_3}{d\bar{H}^I} + \frac{P_4}{P_1} \frac{dX_4}{d\bar{H}^I} - S - \bar{H}^I \frac{dS}{d\bar{H}^I} \tag{6.21}$$

The solutions for output response and the response of

surplus to a change in the number of hours worked
are given below (the derivations are again at
constant prices):

$$\frac{dX_1}{d\bar{H}^I} = -\frac{f_1 \, k_2^F}{k_1^F} \quad < \quad 0 \tag{6.22}$$

$$\frac{dX_2}{d\bar{H}^I} = \quad f_2 \quad > \quad 0 \tag{6.23}$$

$$\frac{dX_3}{d\bar{H}^I} = \frac{f_3 \, k_2^F \, k_4^d}{k_1^F (k_4^d - k_3^d)} \tag{6.24}$$

$$\frac{dX_4}{d\bar{H}^I} = -\frac{f_4 \, k_2^F \, k_3^d}{k_1^F (k_4^d - k_3^d)} \tag{6.25}$$

$$\frac{dS}{d\bar{H}^I} = -\frac{w^I}{\alpha} \, g' \quad > \quad 0 \tag{6.26}$$

Proposition 6.1: An increase in the number of hours
the indentured labourers work always raises the
amount of surplus generated.
    The above theorem follows from equation (6.26).
This is indeed an extremely interesting result. It
clearly demonstrates that an increase in the number
of hours of work by indentured labour invariably
increased the surplus generated. Thus one way of
generating abnormal profits (over and above the
return r_F) in this system is by increasing work
hours. This particular result arises due to underpayment of labour - specifically a payment below
the value of their marginal product and would not
arise if labour was receiving its fair share,
namely, the value of the marginal product. Surplus
generation in Fiji has often been attributed to
white racism. This unimaginative and non-subtle
explanation is not necessarily required for surplus
generation. Market imperfection as a source of
surplus generation does extremely well as is
evident from Proposition 6.1.
    Historical evidence supporting this result can
be presented. It is fascinating to note that the
number of hours worked were increased arbitrarily

97

over time - in direct violation of the contract signed by the indentured labourers.[12] To quote extensively from Gillion(4) page 108, a noted historian of the Fiji indians:

> The day of the immigrants started at 3 or 4 a.m. when they were woken by the mill whistle and the sirdars. They would bathe, cook their breakfast and lunch, and at 4 or 5 a.m. would be mustered with their tools. Those who pleaded sickness were sent for medical treatment. Employers did not invariably make the women work, not the men during the slack season, and there were always a few habitual loafers, criminals, gamblers and prostitutes, who preferred gaol to work. After the muster the Indians set off for the field, the women carrying their infants and lunch in their arms, sacks on their heads (for the children to lie on in the field) and hoes over their shoulders. The maximum distance immigrants could legally be made to walk to work without compensation in the form of a reduced task was two miles. When they arrived at the field at about 5 or 6 a.m., they were alloted their task for the day by the overseers and sirdars, who carried measuring ropes for this purpose. The immigrants usually worked in gangs under a sirdar, the women in a separate gang but the tasks were individually assessed. On a sugar plantation the work consisted of digging or clearing drains and planting, weeding, trashing, cutting and loading cane; in earlier years there were shovel-ploughing tasks also, but later horses were used instead. The size of the task depended on the nature of the soil and the state of the cane, and allowance was made for the inexperienced immigrants. The determination of a fair task was an expert question to be decided in each case; even when there were inspectors of immigrants, the overseers still had considerable latitude.

> Were the task excessive? It will be recalled that the statutory task was the amount of work an immigrant could do in six hours steady work. Tasks could seldom be completed in this time, except by the strongest workers; in practice employers made the hours of task work the same as those of time work (nine hours). It is true that some Indians speak with pride today of how

they would leave for home by noon or 1 p.m., and even earlier, or stay to assist others to finish their tasks, but these were the stronger men. The majority could not leave until 3 or 4 p.m., or even later, occasionally after dark, though some of these had taken several breaks apart from that allowed for lunch. Although of the agricultural classes, they had not been used to working such regular hours with constant muscular effort, but accustomed rhythm and forced pace of plantation work was to produce tensions and difficulties akin to those experience by newcomers to industrial towns.

In the nineteenth century the employers apparently disregarded the legal definition of a task. Managers and overseers were judged on their ability to obtain maximum production at minimum cost, and bonuses were given for economical production, leading to rivalry between estate managers, overseers, and sirdars. Often the only way to reduce costs was to economise on labour, and the immigrants suffered through the resulting 'speed up'.

Thus, historical evidence clearly supports the view that the number of hours worked by indentured labourers were increased in violation of the conditions of the original contract. Proposition 6.1 attributes the above result to the desire to generate a surplus - make abnormal profits. As is well known such profits may arise in situations of market imperfections. In the model outlined such imperfections arise due to asymmetrical distribution of information, resulting in a payment to workers below the value of their marginal product.
   Finally, the welfare consequences of an increase in the hours worked by indentured labourers may be examined. By substituting equations (6.22), (6.23), (6.24) and (6.25) in equation (6.21) and simplifying:

$$\frac{1}{U_1} \frac{dU}{d\bar{H}^I} = w^I - \frac{S}{P_1} - \frac{\bar{H}^I}{P_1} \frac{dS}{d\bar{H}^I} \qquad (6.27)$$

The above expression is of an ambiguous sign. We know that :

$$w^I > 0 \text{ and } dS/d\bar{H}^I > 0$$

therefore the sign of:

$$(1/U_1) \quad dU/d\bar{H}^I$$

is indeterminate. The ambiguity of the above
expression can be explained along the following
lines. The last two expressions in equation (6.27)
capture the effect of an increase in the number of
hours worked by indentured labour on surplus
generated which is taken out of the country as part
of repatriation payment. This invariably has a
negative impact on the welfare of the colony. The
term w^I represents the gain to the economy on account
of the increased production of commodity X_2 due to
the increased number of hours worked (which in a
sense is the same as an increase in the supply of an
indigenous factor). The welfare effect depends on
whether this gain outweights the loss arising from an
increase in the repatriation payments.

In some ways the result contained in equation
(6.27) is quite disturbing. Consider the case in
which:

$$(1/U_1) \quad dU/d\bar{H}^I \quad > \quad 0$$

In this case the plantation owners are quite
satisfied because their return has increased due to
increased exploitation. National welfare has also
increased because it has been assumed that:

$$w^I \quad > \quad S/p_1 + (\bar{H}^I) \quad dS/d\bar{H}^I$$

In such a situation no local support could be
generated for ending the exploitation of the
indentured labour.

It is not surprising (to quote again form
historical records) that the demands for abolition
of indentured labour generally came from outside of
Fiji (except by exploited workers themselves). The
criticisms were voiced by individual scholars and
by several notable Indians. Reverend Burton (2)
in 1910 described the indentured labour system as
barbarous. "Interestingly the book roused a storm
of protest in Fiji" according to Gillion. Gillion
also noted that in March 1912 Gokhale moved a
resolution in Legislative Council for abolition of
the indentured system. These protests are
consistent with the result contained in equation
(6.27).

100

NOTES

1. See for example Gillion (4) and Lal (6) for this figure.
2. The term 'Girmit' means the agreement under which the immigrants came. It has also been interpreted as the indenture experience.
3. It is important to point out that the condition of indentured labourers is compared with some representative labourer in India. This appears to be a good example of injudicious usage of counter-factuals. The workers condition should be compared with either those in Fiji doing similar work or with a competitive wage which under certain conditions may be regarded as a fair return. A good critique of counterfactual history is available in Gerschenkron (3).
4. This passage is taken from Gillion (4) page 107.
5. This quotation is again taken from Gillion (4) page 113.
6. It is not difficult to set up such a model. However, this has not been attempted because this is not the main task of this chapter.
7. It is difficult to obtain an estimate of the wage earned by indentured labourers in India before migrating. The only evidence available is in the profiles of some workers given in Lal's (6) work. He provides a profile of seven workers. In these profiles, for example, Hira Singh earns Rs.2-8-0 a month. The contract for indentured labour shows that these workers were paid on the following basis: "When employed at time-work every able-bodied adult male emigrant above the age of fifteen years will be paid not less than one shilling, which is equal to ten annas, and every other emigrant above the age of ten years not less than nine pence, which is equal to seven annas and two pice, for every working day of nine hours; children below the age of ten years receive wages proportionate to the amount of work done". For an adult worker the monthly wage comes to: (10 x 30)/16 = Rs.18-7 a month which is nine fold greater than the wage in India. By looking at these figures one may be inclined to argue that the indentured labourers were not exploited. However, this is not the correct comparison to make. This must be made with the value of the marginal product of the workers. Let us also add that some economists may even refuse to accept the value of marginal product as a fair wage. I do not dispute this particular position, however,

for modelling purposes the value of marginal product does provide an extremely useful reference point.

8. This sort of underpayment also arises in the case of monopoly. The factors receive marginal revenue product rather than the value of their marginal product - see for example Robinson (8). Robinson defines this underpayment as a form of exploitation.

9. India was regarded as a source of cheap labour. Sir Arthur Gordon, governor of the Colony (Fiji) (1875-1880) made the following statement:

> The supply of labour to be obtained from India is practically boundless. The amount of wages ordinarily given to Indian coolies is well known. I hold in my hand some statistics as to the probable expense of their introduction here. My calculations are £3.18s for recruiting; 10s a head per man for the agent; passage money £12; cost of returning same, £3; in all £19.8s. Deducting from this the amount of one-third, as paid by the Government, we arrive at the fact that, for £12.18.8, we obtain a coolie servant for five years, with his wages of 5d. per day additional, with rations. The West Indian system of immigration which works well, is this: Before a certain day in the year each planter sends in a requisition to the immigration agent, stating the number of coolies he requires for the coming year. These are added up together, and the total they amount to is sent for from India. The men when they arrive are assigned by lot to the applicants, so that there may be no complaints of unfair play. If a number less than that asked for is sent, a proportional diminution in the number allotted is made all round. An indenture fee, in some colonies £1, in others £2, is paid by the planter on each man allotted to him, and a like amount in each succeeding year of the five for which the coolie is indentured to him. The remainder of the expenses, so far as the planter's share of it is concerned (for the Government bears one-third) is defrayed by means of an export duty on produce, which varies every year, according as the number of immigrants sent for it great or small. It must be remembered, when speaking on this subject, that the Indian labourer enters upon his service for a much longer period than the Polynesian. He is engaged to work upon the estate for one certain in five years,

together with an additional five of labour in the
Colony, though not necessarily on the same
estate, before he is entitled to receive a return
passage to the place whence he came. Thus it will
be seen a Polynesian would have to be returned
and re-engaged three times for every time an
Indian labourer would be. The expenses of this
may easily be calculated, and the saving soon
arrived at. I must, however, candidly point out
that, in one respect, the contract of Indian
labourers contrasts unfavourably with those of
Polynesia - that of wages; 5d. per diem,
with rations, was the least amount they could be
maintained at, and without rations they would
cost 10d. per diem. If we had both systems of
immigration at work, the Government would send
for such a number of Polynesians and such a
number of Indians as the planters might
respectively ask for. It would depend on themselves which they would have, and no doubt they
would ask for that which on the whole they found
most advantageous for them. The immediate
question then is, "Is it in your opinion
desirable that efforts should be made to effect
the introduction of immigrant labour from
India" and to this also I would ask you to return
and answer".
10. It is unusual to quote poetry in this type
of work. A lot of prose can also be quoted in
support of this position, however, poetry brings
out this point of view more clearly and dramatically.
These passages of poetry are from Lal (5) and (6).
11. It is interesting that examples of such
asymmetries in information sets can also be given
from more recent times. A good example is
information given to some expatriates at the time of
hiring by the University of the South Pacific.
Prospective employees are often told that it is
difficult to find jobs for spouses, but they are not
told that in fact it is almost impossible to find
jobs for spouses due to government restrictions on
work permits.
12. Narayan (7) attributes the increase in
working hours to fall in the price of sugar. He
states "Though never a part of the contract, the
'task' work was already in operation since 1882.
But with the slump in the sugar price, the employers
turned to over-tasking. And since most workers
could not complete the so-called six-hour task work
even in the usual nine hours, the net result was
that employers greatly increased their productivity

while at the same time paying proportionately lower wages in respect of uncompleted tasks. Therefore what was a fixed wage under the contract now became the maximum which a worker could actually earn, and it was mainly this feature, which spread quickly throughout the plantation system, that contributed directly and significantly to the expansion of the Fiji sugar industry until 1920. Yet, as we shall see below, this was the very feature which sounded the death-knell to the plantation system in Fiji". Two observations are in order regarding the above passage. First, the contract was never written in terms of a fixed real wage. The nominal wage was fixed and therefore the real wage was a variable quite clearly from the contract. Second, Narayan's passage does not make any sense unless one has a model which defines exploitation formally and links it to generation of surplus. Differentiation of equation (6.7) shows that:

$$\frac{dS}{dp_2} = (1 - \alpha) (f_2 - k_2^F f_2') > 0$$

which implies that whenever the price of commodity 2 fell the surplus declined. One way of making it up was to overtask labour - this is what Narayan is hinting at in the above passage.

REFERENCES

(1) Akerloff, G. 1970. The Market for Lemons: Qualitative Uncertainty and the Market Mechanism. *Quarterly Journal of Economics*, Vol.84 (August) 488-50.
(2) Burton, J.W. 1910. *The Fiji of Today*. London.
(3) Gerschenkron, A. 1968. *Continuity in History and Other Essays*. Cambridge, Massachusetts: The Belknap Press.
(4) Gillion, K.L. 1973. *Fiji's Indian Migrants. A History to the end of Indenture in 1920*. Melbourne: Melbourne University Press.
(5) Lal, B.V. 1980. Approaches to the Study of Indian Indentured Emigration, with Special Refererence to Fiji. *Journal of Pacific History*, Vol.15 (January) 52-70.
(6)————— 1980. *Leaves of the Banyan Tree*. Unpublished PhD Thesis, Australian National University.
(7) Narayan, J. 1976. *Fiji - A Case Study in Political Economy*. Unpublished PhD Thesis, The University of Alberta.

(8) Robinson, J. 1933. *The Economics of Imperfect Competition*. London: Macmillan and Company-

(9) Sanderson Committee Report (1909): Committee on Emigration from India.

AUTHOR INDEX